WE BELIEVE

EXPERIENCING THE NICENE CREED THROUGH ANCIENT AFRICAN CHRISTIANITY

VOLUME 2

CHRISTOPHER A HALL

Copyright © 2025 by ICCS PRESS, INC, Christopher A. Hall
Published by ICCS Press, 616 Prospect Street, New Haven, CT 06511 www.iccspress.com

All rights reserved. No part of this book may be reproduced in any form or by any electronic or mechanical means, including information storage and retrieval systems, without written permission from ICCS Press, except for the use of brief quotations in a book review.

Cover Design: Gina Peterson, Speers Design Associates, LLC.

Cover Image: *Epiphany* by Yoseph Abate. https://fineartamerica.com/profiles/yoseph-abate

Library of Congress Cataloging-in-Publication Data
Hall, Christopher A.
We Believe: Experiencing the Creed through Ancient African Christianity: Volume Two
Christopher A. Hall.
ISBN: 978-1-62428-041-2 AMAZON;
978-1-62428-042-9 PB; 978-1-62428-043-6 Kindle

CONTENTS

1. Introduction — 1
2. Light from Light — 42
3. True God — 51
4. Begotten, not Made — 55
5. One with the Father — 83
6. For Us — 91
7. Our Salvation — 105
8. From Heaven — 113
9. By Power — 129
10. Incarnation — 138
11. Virgin Birth — 157

About the Author — 181
Cover Artist — 183

1
INTRODUCTION

We believe in one Lord, Jesus Christ, the only Son of God, eternally begotten of the Father, God from God.

Welcome to Volume Two of *We Believe,* the second volume in my series on the Nicene Creed and the contribution of the African church fathers to its formation. I expect to write five volumes.

Each volume is also available in four shorter books of about fifty pages from ICCS Press. Four books have been incorporated into each volume, with significant editing and occasional additions and deletions.

Take a close look at the title for the entire series: *We Believe: Experiencing the Creed through Ancient African Christianity.*[1] It's important. We not only want to learn about the Nicene Creed, but we also want to enter it experientially. We want the Creed to form not only our minds, but our souls.

In Volume One I discussed a number of important issues. We especially considered "God the Father," whom the Creed describes as "Almighty, maker of heaven and earth, of all that is, seen and unseen." We also considered the nature of belief and the importance of the Bible as the foundation for all that we believe about God.

---

1. The phrase "experiencing the Creed through Ancient Christianity" comes from Gary Moon. I am indebted to Gary for the phrase. You'll find it occasionally in his writing.

The Nicene Creed was written in 325 CE at Nicaea, a relatively small city in what today is the nation of Turkey. Church fathers gathered in "council" from around the Mediterranean basin, the geographical area surrounding the Mediterranean Sea. The southern rim of the basin is North Africa, what today includes countries such as Algeria, Morocco, Tunisia, Libya, and Egypt.

Church leaders from Northern Africa, such as the African church father Augustine, clearly considered themselves as "African." They were also members of the Roman Empire or "Roman." Their first allegiance, however, was to Africa. They were Africans and proud of the fact.

To travel to Nicaea, some African leaders sailed across the Mediterranean Sea. Note the movement: south to north. Not only did Africans attending the Council of Nicaea travel from south to north, but so did their thoughts. Key theological ideas followed this south-north trajectory, from the late first century CE. African insights continued to do so for years after the Council of Nicaea had completed its work.

Other African church fathers, wary of crossing the sea, traveled around the edge of the Mediterranean, first heading east, then north across countries such as Israel and Syria, and finally west to Nicaea. It was a daunting, exhausting journey. But the Christian leaders gathering in Nicaea knew that the council would be debating and deciding essential issues and formulating key doctrines for the church. Sacrifice, courage, worship, prayer, wisdom and perseverance would be required.

Of course, the ideas, insights, wisdom and practices of the African church fathers at Nicaea weren't created suddenly out of whole cloth. African fathers gathered at Nicaea had carefully considered the thoughts, lives, and worship of those who lived before them. Tertullian and Origen, for instance, were Africans who lived in the second and third centuries CE, yet made important contributions that later church fathers in the fourth century carefully pondered. For example, Tertullian's writings concerning the Trinity were prescient.

There were important issues to discuss and decide at Nicaea, all of them related to what God had done for his precious image-bearers in the birth, life, death, resurrection, and ascension of Jesus Christ. In Volume Two, we will focus on Christ as the Son of God who enters the world on our behalf.

I suggest that readers unfamiliar with the We Believe series, consult either Volume One, or the four shorter books. If this is not possible for you, I'll review occasionally material that you'll find in Volume One.

In Volume Two, the book that you hold in your hands, I look closely at the first phrase of the Nicene Creed's next line:

We believe in one Lord, Jesus Christ, the only Son of God, eternally begotten of the Father, God from God...

Read slowly this phrase of the Nicene Creed. What questions or concerns come to mind? Consider the following two questions, both related to the first seven words: "We believe in one Lord, Jesus Christ..."

- Why does the Nicene Creed state the church believes in only "one Lord"?

- When the Nicene fathers proclaimed Jesus as "Lord", what did they mean?

These two questions are very important. If we answer them well, our faith will be significantly strengthened. This will take some time. There is no need to rush.

TO AFFIRM "ONE LORD" CAN BE COSTLY

We must remember that to declare "one Lord" in the Roman world was often a very costly affirmation for ancient Christians, and continues to be so for many modern believers.

Ancient Christians affirmed that there is "one Lord", not many Lords. To express unwavering loyalty to only one Lord can be costly and demanding as we live in the midst of this present evil age (*Gal* 1:4), a time when many lords and authorities demand our allegiance.

* * *

Pause and reflect: Have there been times when you have experienced opposition or persecution for your faithfulness and commitment to Christ as the one Lord? Has anyone ever said to you, "How can Jesus be the only way to God? That's fine for you, but not for me. Why are you being so exclusive?" How did you respond? Did you find the experience encouraging or discouraging?

* * *

To declare "Jesus is Lord" in Africa during the lifetime of ancient Christians like Origen, Tertullian, and Cyprian entailed the ever-present possibility of significant suffering and death. Origen writes, "We have learned from the Gospel neither to relax our efforts in times of peace or to give ourselves up to leisure, nor, when the world makes war upon us, to become cowards and apostatize from the love of the God of all things, who is Jesus Christ."[2]

The Roman government struggled to understand why sacrifice to the emperor's divinity posed such a problem for the Christian community. This sacrifice was considered by most Romans as simply a sign of political loyalty to Caesar. Indeed, except for a few mentally imbalanced emperors – Caligula comes to mind – most emperors realized they weren't divine. The claim, though, served as an effective means of unifying the Roman Empire and identifying possible traitors.

The Romans were largely tolerant of other religions. They were willing to add Jesus to the pantheon of Roman gods. To add another god made little difference to Rome. To claim that Jesus was the only god, however, made all the difference in the world; such a claim smelled of arrogance, obstinacy, and treason to Caesar.

Rome simply didn't understand the obstinacy (Lat. *obstinacia*) of Christians and their determination to worship Jesus as the one and only Lord. From a Roman perspective, the refusal to sacrifice to the emperor's divinity was viewed as evidence of political, cultural, and religious disloyalty to Rome, its values, and its gods. Though harsh persecution was sporadic, when it occurred it was brutal and violent.

The Romans depended on the gods for good weather, fertile lands, healthy families, political stability, and military success. When disasters

---

2. Origen, *Against Celsus*, ANF 4.440. The letters ANF stand for "Ante Nicene Fathers", a 10-volume set published by Hendrickson. The reference, then, refers to Volume 4, page 440, of the ANF.

struck, the Romans suspected religious disloyalty as their cause. Tertullian comments: "They think the Christians the cause of every public disaster, of every affliction with which the people are visited. If the Tiber rises as high as the city walls, if the Nile does not send its waters up over the fields, if the heavens give no rain, if there is an earthquake, if there is famine or pestilence, immediately the cry is, 'Away with the Christians to the lion.'"[3]

The great North African biblical scholar Origen suffered for his faith in "one Lord." As a young man, Origen witnessed his own father's martyrdom, and at the end of his life Origen suffered severely at the hands of the Roman government.

The church historian Eusebius relates "how many and of what nature were the sufferings which the man [Origen] endured for the word of Christ, bonds and tortures of the body, and torments under iron and in the recesses of a prison, and how for a great many days, with his feet stretched four spaces in that instrument of torture – the stocks – he steadfastly bore threats of fire, and all other things inflicted by his enemies."[4] Finally released, Origen's injuries proved too great, and Origen's mind and heart were lost to the church.

The martyrs' faithful and courageous witness demonstrates clearly that ancient African Christian faith was much more than an intellectual exercise and affirmation. The same is true for Christ's modern African disciples. When Africans affirm the Nicene Creed's sentences, they too proclaim their willingness to live – and die – for its teachings.

In Northern Africa today, and in sub-Saharan Africa, to affirm there is only "one Lord" is a dangerous, even seditious act. Many have paid with their lives and continue to do so for their loyalty to Jesus. This ultimate sacrifice faithfully emulates the willingness of ancient African Christians to stain African soil with the blood of heartfelt witness.

Thomas Oden comments that the "rapid spread of early African Christianity was due in part to the heartbreaking African history of martyrdom. This is a history of African blood on African soil. For African believers the martyrs pointed to the continuity of the communion of the saints. They bore their cross in Africa. They evoked a luminous awareness

---

3. Tertullian, *Apology* 40.2.
4. Eusebius, *Ecclesiastical History* 6.10.

of their relation with esteemed ancestors. That is very intuitively African."[5]

Perhaps even more important for our study of the African church fathers and the formation of the Nicene Creed, Oden observes that it "was amid that period of martyrdom that the teachings of African orthodoxy were decisively refined. It was in that context that Africa gave birth to the enduring doctrines of creation, providence, sin, atonement, resurrection, and the church – its liturgy, eucharistic life, teaching, and discipleship, refined by the fires of African experience."[6]

THE CHURCH BELIEVES IN ONE LORD, NOT MANY

Paul's words *in First Corinthians* explain why the church clearly declared its belief in only "one Lord" in the Nicene Creed. Read them carefully:

> Hence, as to the eating of food offered to idols, we know that 'no idol in the world really exists,' and that 'there is no God but one.' Indeed, even though there may be so-called gods in heaven or on earth – as in fact there are many gods and many lords – yet for us there is one God, the Father, from whom are all things and for whom we exist, and one Lord, Jesus Christ, through whom are all things and through whom we exist. It is not everyone, however, who has this knowledge. Since some have become so accustomed to idols until now, they still think of the food they eat as food offered to an idol; and their conscience, being weak, is defiled (1 *Cor* 8:4-7, NRSV).

Did you notice how Paul attests "one God, the Father," and then affirms "one Lord Jesus Christ"? How does he describe the Father? ". . . from whom are all things and for whom we exist." How does he describe the "one Lord"? " . . . through whom are all things and through whom we exist." The African fathers delighted in exploring this mutual relationship between the Father and the "one Lord, Jesus Christ."

It is against the background of idolatry in the ancient world that Paul's

---

5. Thomas C. Oden, *How Africa Shaped the Christian Mind: Rediscovering the African Seedbed of Western Christianity* (Downers Grove: IVP, 2007), 117.
6. Ibid., 120.

words resound. There is only one God – the Father. There is only one Lord -- Jesus Christ. In Paul's world, "not everyone" possessed this knowledge.

The same could be said of Africa today. Certain African religious beliefs and practices contradict this line of the Creed; magic, witchcraft, child sacrifice, and calling on the ancestors to intervene come to mind.[7]

* * *

Pause and reflect: To be a Christian is to affirm one's trust in "one Lord," not many, and to say a firm "no" to the temptation to turn to idols or ancestors to attain power that we may be unconvinced the "one Lord" possesses. Have you ever been tempted to do so? When we affirm our faith in "one Lord," we declare our trust in the character and power of Jesus as that "one Lord". Try to identify specific instances where the affirmation of "one Lord" was difficult for you. What was the nature of the difficulty? How did you respond?

* * *

Kwame Bediako captures well the African perspective on Jesus as the "one Lord" and the power of Christ over Satan and the kingdom of evil. He observes that Africans readily acknowledge "ubiquitous forces and mysterious powers," but also strongly affirm that "the Christian who has understood that Jesus Christ is a living reality, can be at home, assured in the faith that *Jesus alone is Lord*, Protector, Provider and Enabler. In the struggles and battles of life, the Christian discovers that Jesus goes ahead, and that . . . .he alone is capable of fighting and conquering, leading his people in triumph."[8]

---

7. Joe M. Kapolyo comments that "Africans are very spiritual. Unlike their Western counterparts, they have no need to be convinced of the existence of God. Many are even monotheistic. Both the humanist rationalism that characterizes the West and the atheistic materialism that sums up communism are foreign to the African mind." Joe M. Kapolyo, *The Human Condition: Christian Perspectives through African Eyes* (Downers Grove: InterVarsity Press, 2005), 122.
8. Kwame Bediako, *Jesus and the Gospel in Africa* (Maryknoll, NY: Orbis Books, 2004), 9; my emphasis.

JESUS IS THE ONE LORD

Jesus was a Jewish man who was born in Judea in roughly 5 BCE. He grew up in a Jewish family. As a growing boy he learned Hebrew and Aramaic, and studied in the synagogue. He worshiped at the religious festivals in Jerusalem and observed the Jewish religious calendar. He came to be recognized as a public teacher. Some Jews called him "Rabbi."

Yet Jesus was not only a Jewish man. He was and is God incarnate as the "one Lord". The word "Lord," "*Kyrios*" in Greek and "*dominus*" in Latin, is an important word that teaches us much about Jesus' status as the Son of God. For instance, when the Hebrew Bible was translated into Greek in the fourth century BCE for the sake of Jews who read Greek much better than Hebrew, the Greek word *Kyrios* was chosen to translate *Yahweh*, the highest and holiest name for God in Hebrew. The Latin word *dominus* was chosen as its Latin equivalent, a term often used for the Roman emperor from Augustus on.

When Jesus is identified in the Nicene Creed as *Kyrios*, then, the Creed is affirming as a statement of Christian belief that Jesus is the incarnation of *Yahweh*, the God of Israel. He exists eternally as the Son of God, and in the fulness of time enters the world as a human being.

Jesus himself believed that he was God, a completely ridiculous affirmation if not true. How would you respond to a modern person who claimed to be God? Probably with a chuckle rather than faith and belief. Yet in John 8, at the end of a long, heated debate with Jewish religious leaders, Jesus makes this very claim: "Very truly I tell you, before Abraham was, I am" (*Jn* 8:58). "I am" (*ego eimi* in Greek), reflects Jesus' own self-understanding that *Yahweh* and he are identical, yet still distinct. How this is possible is something we will continually explore in the *We Believe* series on the Nicene Creed.

In John 8, Jesus also is saying something important about his relationship to time. *He was present with Abraham.* And now he is present to the nation of Israel as their incarnate Lord. "Your ancestor Abraham rejoiced that he would see my day; he saw it and was glad" (*Jn* 8:56).

Without doubt, the Jewish leaders understood what Jesus was claiming, for "they picked up stones to throw at him" (*Jn* 8:59). From their perspective, Jesus was blaspheming. He was lying about God. Yet Jesus didn't back down. God the eternal Son had now come to Israel in a new, unexpected way as "Lord" -- the incarnation of *Yahweh*. God is drawing closer to Israel than ever before.

The Latin *dominus* is also significant as a title for Jesus, for every person living in North Africa and the rest of the Mediterranean world acknowledged Caesar as *dominus*. To a Roman, *Dominus* surely had a political meaning, and often a religious one.

In the Nicene Creed, the church declared that Jesus Christ is "Lord", not Caesar. To proclaim this was a treasonous act, and many Christians died as a result of their faithfulness to their "Lord." Countless numbers experienced martyrdom in the first centuries of the church's history, right up to the conversion of Constantine around 312 CE. Not only so, but Christians died for an incarnate God who had been crucified by Rome. Tom Holland, well-known historian of the Roman world, comments: "That a man who had himself been crucified might be hailed as a god could not help but been seen by people everywhere across the Roman world as scandalous, obscene, grotesque."[9]

FULLY HUMAN, FULLY DIVINE

If Jesus is fully divine, he also is fully human, with all the characteristics a human male possesses. Ancient Christians debated the question of Jesus' human nature for years, and finally a consensus was reached at Nicaea. Jesus is both "human" and "divine."

The African fathers understood that Jesus must be *fully human* and *fully divine* to accomplish his redemptive work. Clement of Alexandria calls his readers to believe "in him who is *man and God*," "who suffered and is worshiped as the living God," "who is the only God of all humankind. Believe and receive salvation for your reward."[10]

Cyril of Alexandria, writing years later, reinforces Clement's teaching. Cyril directs our attention to *Philippians* 2:9. In the incarnation of the Son of God, the Father gives the Son "the name that is above every name." As the Son willingly enters our world with the birth of Jesus at Bethlehem, he

---

9. Tom Holland, *Dominion: How the Christian Revolution Remade the World* (New York: Basic Books, 2019), 6.
10. Clement of Alexandria, *Exhortation to the Greeks* 10. (106); ACD 2.3. (*Ancient Christian Doctrine*), Vol. 2, page 3); my emphasis.

"took the name of a servant and assumed our poverty and low estate."[11] Yet he never ceased being God. This would be an impossibility, for God can't stop being God.

When Christ completed his redemptive work, Cyril writes, "he was raised to the glory that belonged to him by nature," "to that which was his own" as the Son of God before the incarnation.[12] This is the glory of the one Lord. "For, existing before the ages and before the worlds, as one that was of God and was God, he was clothed with the glory that belongs to the Godhead."[13]

The incarnation of the eternal Son involved no "mutation nor change" in the Son's divine nature. He "continued rather in that state in which he had constantly existed..."[14]

Note carefully what Cyril is saying. When the Son becomes a human being – Jesus of Nazareth --he never ceases to be God, the one Lord. As Cyril puts it, "he endured neither mutation nor change."[15] Again, *God can't stop being God*, incarnate or not.

Still, with Jesus' birth from the Virgin Mary, the Son of God becomes fully human. After his birth, Jesus is *simultaneously* fully human and fully God. Only God can save from sin and only a human can die for sins. Hence, Jesus must be both. He is not some third thing, partly God and partly human, for such a creature could help no one.

So, everything we predicate of God, we proclaim to be true of Jesus. And everything we predicate of a human male, we proclaim to be true of Jesus. The incarnate Christ is *both* omniscient, *and* constantly learning. He is omnipresent, fully present everywhere in the universe, while he lived for many years in Israel, fully present there in his incarnate body.

How can Jesus be both human and divine? When we encounter the wonder of the incarnation, we meet an incomprehensible mystery. We affirm and worship the mystery, but never comprehend it.

The heresies we will find clustered around the doctrine of the incarnation are invariably attempts to eliminate the logical tension this mystery

---

11. Cyril of Alexandria, *Homilies on the Gospel of Luke* 128; ACD 2.4.
12. Ibid.
13. Ibid.
14. Ibid.
15. Ibid.

produces; they reduce this tension either by emphasizing Jesus' deity at the expense of his humanity, or vice versa.

When we attempt to resolve the logical tension that the mystery of the incarnation presents, we endanger the gospel. Why? Only God can save, for sin is always an offense against God (cf. *Ps* 51:4). And only this human male can die for our sin. God saves, then, by entering history in the person of the eternal Son, who joins his divine nature to the human nature offered to him by the Virgin Mary in an inexpressible, incomprehensible union.

WITHOUT SIN

Was Jesus' human nature infected with sin like ours? If not, how could he be genuinely human? He wouldn't be, if sin is an essential aspect of human nature as created by God. But it isn't. Rather, sin is like a cancer that feeds off human nature. It is a contagion that has infected human nature. Augustine called sin a *privatio boni,* a privation of good. What does Augustine mean?

Augustine teaches that sin is like a disease, a contamination or infestation that infects all human beings. Picture sin as a hole in a piece of cloth that gradually widens until the entire cloth unravels. Or think of a good steak left out in the sun. What happens? Soon flies descend upon the meat and lay their eggs. In a short time, maggots appear and begin to consume the steak. Rot progressively spoils or corrupts the entire piece of meat. Or think of decay in a tooth. The same principle applies. Untreated decay will finally consume a tooth.

Once the hole or the rot or decay have accomplished their destructive work, the cloth has unraveled, the meat has decomposed, and the tooth has decayed; what happens to the hole or rot or decay when their corrupted work is accomplished? They disappear. Similarly, sin is an infestation or infection that corrupts or infects human nature and, left to itself, destroys it. But it is not an inherent aspect of human nature as created by God.

Thankfully, the human nature Jesus received from Mary wasn't corrupt or infected like ours. It was not polluted by sin's contamination. The eternal Son's divine nature, in union with the perfect human nature offered to him by Mary, protected and preserved Jesus' human nature from the contagion of sin.

So, if you want to see what a real human being looks like – one that corresponds to God's original blueprint – *look at Jesus*. Jesus represents what we were created to be: a healthy, whole, flawless, perfect human being.[16]

HOW CAN THIS BE?

Only Jesus of Nazareth is both fully human and fully divine. He is utterly unique. Clement of Alexandria writes, "He alone is both God and man."[17] Ancient Christians struggled to understand how this could be true, as you might also be wondering. How can divinity and humanity be fully true of a single person?

An Egyptian presbyter named Arius tried to solve this problem. He taught that Jesus was a highly exalted creature, but not God. From Arius's perspective, a human being could not be God if the unity or oneness of God was to be preserved. That is, if God is one, God could not be three. This Trinitarian arithmetic made little sense to Arius.

Let's focus on Arius's idea that Jesus was an elevated creature. African leaders such as Athanasius responded that Jesus was no mere creature, however elevated he may be. For it would be blasphemous to worship a creature. And, as Athanasius insisted, a human being can't save other humans from sin. Only God can save from sin and the havoc sin wreaks on human lives.

Athanasius refers to a number of biblical texts to make his point. The followers of Arius, viewing Jesus as an exalted creature, faced a series of texts in the first chapter of Hebrews that undermined their position, and Athanasius knew they did.

* * *

Pause and reflect: Before reading the next paragraph, take a moment to

---

16. I develop these ideas in greater depth in Christopher A. Hall, *A Different Way: Recentering the Christian Life Around Following Jesus* (San Francisco: Harper One, 2023), 87-93.
17. Clement of Alexandria, *Exhortation to the Greeks* 1.7; ACD 2.14.

read *Hebrews* 1. List three texts that indicate that Jesus is God, and not a creature such as an angel.

* * *

The writer of Hebrews insists that the Son is not an angel, but superior to the angels. "And again, when God brings his firstborn into the world, he says, 'Let all God's angels worship him,'" a text the writer quotes from Deuteronomy 32:43. Athanasius insists that the writer's point is clear. "He would not have been worshiped or spoken of in this way if he belonged merely to the rank of creatures."[18] For worshiping a creature would be blasphemy.

Athanasius concludes that whatever it means for God to have a Son or for God to be his Father, *one thing must be beyond dispute*: this is "an offspring proper to his substance and a Son by nature."[19] Hence, the divine nature of the Son explains "why he is worshiped and is believed to be God . . . For it is proper to the Son to have all that the Father has and to be such that the Father is beheld in him, and that through him all things were made and that in him the salvation of all is brought about and is established."[20]

The Father "is beheld in" the Son. If you want to get a good look at what God is like, look at Jesus, the incarnate Lord. Jesus encourages the disciples to do this very thing in John 14:9. "Anyone who has seen me has seen the Father."

* * *

Pause and reflect: Some readers might want to take a year or two and simply read the Gospels again and again. Immerse your mind in Jesus' words and actions. Go slow. Chew on the text like a cow chews on its cud. Slowly Jesus' mind will slip into your mind. Your mental habit patterns will wrap themselves around those of Jesus. You'll begin to see your world and your life differently. Keep a journal and record insights as they come.

---

18. Athanasius, *Against the Arians* 2.24; ACD 2.24-25.
19. Ibid; ACD 2.25.
20. Ibid.

* * *

A commonplace in the ancient Roman world was the Latin phrase, *Repetitio mater studiorum est.* "Repetition is the mother of all learning." A Roman or North African tutor insisted that his students repeat their lessons again and again. Roman tutors knew that deep change occurs slowly, and that a well-developed memory was essential if one was to develop an educated, mature mind.

So, as you study with me in the *We Believe* series, I'll occasionally encourage you to memorize something. For instance, try this sentence on for size: "Jesus is fully God and fully human." As you memorize it, ponder it carefully. Everything we say about God, we can say about Jesus. Simultaneously, though, Jesus possesses every characteristic of a human male. As you meditate on these wonders and beauties, questions and insights will come. Welcome them. Write them down. You'll find yourself growing in your relationship with God.

Athanasius loved the Gospel of John and refers to it often. For instance, Athanasius directs our attention to John 13:13. It reads: "You call me teacher and Lord – and you are right, for that is what I am." Jesus is the disciples' teacher and their divine Lord. Though "Lord" can simply be a term of respect in *koine* Greek, something like "Sir" or "Master", it possesses a deeper meaning for John and for Jesus. We perceive this meaning as Thomas encounters Jesus after the resurrection.

Do you remember that Thomas doubted that Jesus had risen from the dead? Thomas had not been present at Jesus' first appearance to the apostles, and refused to believe. Jesus appeared to the disciples again when Thomas was present, and invited Thomas to place his finger in the nail holes in his hands, and the lance wound in his side. "Do not doubt but believe" (*Jn* 20:27). Thomas's doubt dissolved and he readily affirmed his belief in Jesus as God. "My Lord and my God" (*Jn* 20:28). Jesus as Thomas's "Lord", then, is Thomas's "God." How this can be true is an incomprehensible wonder, verified by Jesus' resurrection from the dead. The living Lord – God incarnate -- is standing in front of Thomas, with the wounds of the crucifixion imprinted on his body.

The incarnation remains incomprehensible because it affirms two truths that are *conceptually impossible* for us to reconcile. Jesus is *both* divine and human, *fully* God and *fully* human.

In Christ, God and human nature join in an incomprehensible union that cannot be comprehended but can be adored. Our constant temptation is to reduce one or other side of the incarnation's mystery in a misplaced attempt to solve the logical conundrum the incarnation poses. If we do so, as the African fathers understood, we undermine the gospel itself.

COROLLARIES TO THE DOCTRINE OF THE INCARNATION

What are some corollaries to the doctrine of the incarnation, things that naturally follow if the incarnation is true? Well, as Origen perceived, if the incarnate Son is God, he must be prior to whatever is created by God. "For the sacred Scriptures know that he is older than all created things and that it was that God who said, concerning the creation of humankind, 'Let us make people after our image and likeness'" (Gen 1:26).[21]

What Origen teaches makes good sense. If the Son, the divine *Logos* (Jn 1:1), is genuinely God, he existed before the creation of the universe, for he created it. He must be "older" than creation. When God says, "Let us make man in our own image" (Gen 1:26), the image in which humans are created is the image of the Son, who is equally God with the Father (*Col* 1:15ff).

Here we discern the deeper, incarnational logic, which can be expressed, though not comprehended. The church fathers speak of the incarnation more in terms of *what it is not than of what it is*. We find the incarnation's deepest, clearest expression in the worship of the church as it proclaims, "and in one Lord, Jesus Christ."

ARIAN CONFUSION

Let's probe a bit more deeply Arian beliefs about Jesus. Arius and those who followed him proclaimed, "He is a creature, but not as one of the creatures; a work, but not as one of the works; an offspring, but not as one of the offsprings."[22] That is to say, Arius believed that Jesus was a creature,

---

21. Origen, *Against Celsus* 5.37; ACD 2.30.
22. Arian teaching as quoted by Athanasius, *Against the Arians* 2.19-20; ACD 2.45.

but unlike any other creature, utterly unique and set apart by the Father who had created him.

Nonetheless, Arius believed Jesus was a creature, not God incarnate. "There was a time when he was not," as a popular Arian slogan puts it. So, if you drew a line in the sand between creatures and their divine creator, the Arians clearly believed Jesus would be on the creature side of the line.

The Arian model of who Jesus is was attractive to some ancient Christians, because it appeared to resolve the conundrums the orthodox model presented. The Arian model answered the question, "how can Jesus be both human and divine?", by denying that he is divine. Problem solved. Athanasius responded, "Not so fast."

For a creature, however elevated it may be, is still a creature. Athanasius saw this clearly. "For though the Son may excel the rest by comparison, yet he remains a creature like them, for among those who are by nature creatures one may find some excelling others."[23] The highest creature is still that, a creature. And creatures cannot save from sin. Nor should we worship them. "But if the whole earth sings the praises of the Creator and the truth, and blesses him and trembles before him, and if its Creator is the Word and he himself says, 'I am the truth' (*Jn* 14:6), then it follows that the Word *is not a creature* but is the sole true Word of the Father. In him all things are set in order, and he himself has his praises sung by all, as Creator."[24]

Those who followed Arius failed to understand or acknowledge the fundamental difference between the Creator and the creature. Athanasius, however, realized that a creature's "being" or "essence" is different from the Creator's. A creature's "being" is derived from something or someone greater than itself.

Not so with the Creator, for the Creator's being is *underived*. Indeed, all "being" is derived from God, who is Being itself. Athanasius rightly sees that the Father and Son share the same "being" or "essence", and are engaged in identical work to save, a truth apparent in a text like John 5:17: "But Jesus answered them, 'My Father is still working, and I am working.'"

* * *

---

23. Ibid.
24. Ibid.

Pause and reflect: Pause for a moment and consider Jesus' words that we've just read from John 5. Jewish religious leaders were outraged that Jesus healed on the Sabbath, a day of rest for Israel. Yet Jesus healed on the Sabbath, and did so because "my Father is still working, and I also am working" (Jn 5:17). Jesus' opponents grasped the implications of Jesus' words; he was claiming to be God. ". . . not only was he breaking the Sabbath, but he was even calling God his own Father, making himself equal with God" (Jn 5:19). Jesus is God incarnate. How might this wondrous truth impact your life more deeply? What steps can you take to increase its influence on your life? Try to name three.

* * *

In response to his Jewish opponents, Jesus didn't back down. Indeed, he raised the ante. He "can do nothing on his own, but only what he sees the Father doing: for whatever the Father does, the Son does likewise" (Jn 5:19).

The Father raises the dead and gives them life. So "also the Son gives life to whomever he wishes" (Jn 5:21). The Father "has given all judgment to the Son, so that all may honor the Son just as they honor the Father. Anyone who does not honor the Son does not honor the Father who sent him" (5:22-23). Just as the Father has life in himself, "so he has granted the Son also to have life in himself" (5:26). The authority to "execute judgment" has been given to Jesus, "because he is the Son of Man" (5:27). In the future "all who are in their graves will hear his voice and will come out – those who have done what is good will rise to live, and those who have done what is evil will rise to be condemned" (5:28-29, NIV).

All these texts from John 5 describe words and actions that characterize God: possessing life in himself, executing judgment, raising the dead, and so on. What is striking is that Jesus claims these divine characteristics for himself, because he is "the Son of Man" or "the Son."

Let's be clear. What Jesus is saying is either blasphemy – he is lying about his relationship to God – or is divinely revealed truth. The Arian model of Jesus as an exalted creature simply doesn't fit what we read in John 5, and African fathers such as Augustine, Cyril of Alexandria, and Athanasius knew this full well.

CHRISTOLOGICAL COACHING FROM AUGUSTINE

Augustine knew John 5 like the back of his hand. He had memorized it. He had meditated on it. He had chewed on it like a cow chews on its cud. And if Jesus' words in John 5 are true, Augustine realized, fully human though Jesus was, he was much more than a human being. For in Jesus, the Creator of the world had stepped into human history.

A few selections from Augustine's comments on John 5 will have to suffice, accompanied by a short comment by me. They come from the *Ancient Christian Commentary on Scripture*:

"Here he has already indicated that *he is equal to God*. 'My Father,' he says, 'is working until now, and I too am working.' . . . . 'And I too am working,' *making himself equal to God* and again they [the Jewish leaders] are disturbed."[25]

This is a key point for Augustine. If the Father is working "until now," and "I too am working," Jesus is claiming to work just like God the Father. The Jewish leaders understand what Jesus is saying, and they are furious.

"Therefore it is as if he said to the Jews, 'Why do you expect that I should not work on the sabbath? The sabbath day was ordained for you as a sign about me. You observe the works of God: I was there when they were made. They were all made by me . . .'"[26]

Jesus is insistent. The sabbath was ordained as a sign by the Father about Jesus, God's Son. The Jewish leaders are well aware that a miracle has occurred with the healing of the paralytic, *yet they fail to discern the message in the miracle*.

Not only so, but Augustine teaches that Jesus did not begin to work on the sabbath when he healed the paralyzed man. No. Jesus as the Word of God -- the *Logos of God* (cf. *Jn* 1:1) -- has been working with his Father from the first moment of creation.

"So," writes Augustine, "the Jews understood what the Arians did not. For the Arians say that the Son is not equal to the father, and hence sprang up that heresy that afflicts the church."[27] This is an amazing irony for Augustine. The Arians, who claimed to be orthodox Christians, failed

---

25. Augustine, *Sermon* 125.6; ACCS NT 4A, John 1-10, edited by Joel C. Elowsky (Downers Grove: IVP Academic, 2006), 186; my emphasis.
26. Augustine, *Tractates on the Gospel of John* 17.15; ACCS NT: 4A.187.
27. Augustine, *Tractates on the Gospel of John* 17.16; ACCS NT: 4A.188.

to see what Jesus' Jewish opponents perceive. The Jewish religious leaders realize what Jesus is claiming, while the Arians – who claimed to follow Jesus – remain blind to the reality of who Jesus is.

"In one sense," Augustine observes, "the Jews were right [about their indignation], because a man dared to make himself *equal to God*. But they were also wrong because they did not understand that it was God in the man. They saw the flesh, but they did not know God. They looked on the dwelling place, but they did not know the dweller. That the flesh was a temple; God dwelt within it."[28]

Augustine repeatedly emphasizes this point. The Jews only saw Jesus, who looked like a man. Indeed, he was and is a human male to this day. Yet the Jewish leaders failed to see that the new "temple" was in their midst, the temple of Jesus' body, for God the Son dwelt within Jesus' humanity.

We have explored what the Nicene Creed says about Jesus as "one Lord." We have seen that this phrase emphasizes that God has entered the history of Israel as the incarnate Son. It is now time to investigate what the name "Jesus Christ" signified to the African fathers.

". . . . JESUS CHRIST. . . "

John McGuckin, editor of *Ancient Christian Doctrine*, Volume Two, helpfully summarizes what the church fathers understood by the name "Jesus Christ." Jesus Christ is "the personal designation of the incarnate Lord," with "Christ generally" signifying the status of the Word of God in the historical condition of the incarnation. Though the title does have "messianic resonances," for the fathers these resonances "were overshadowed by the power of the Logos title to all effects."[29]

The church fathers as a whole, including African fathers, were concerned to refute the ideas of heretics such as Marcion. Marcion argued that the God presented by Old Testament authors couldn't possibly be the God revealed in Jesus.

The church responded to Marcion with a resounding "no," stressing that Jesus as the Christ was surely present in the thoughts and writing of

---

28. Augustine, *Tractates on the Gospel of John* 18.2.1; ACCS NT: 4A.188; my emphasis.
29. John McGuckin, ed., *Ancient Christian Doctrine* 2.11.

inspired prophets such as Moses, Isaiah, and the Old Testament prophetic tradition as a whole.

At the same time, the church fathers realized that the incarnation of God the Son was unexpected and new. As McGuckin puts it, "the incarnation was always received by the church as a radical new beginning. The delicate balancing act of accepting the Old Testament while reinterpreting it strictly through the New was a notable achievement of patristic theology." Indeed, McGuckin believes, the African Cyril of Alexandria's work in this respect "became something of a highwater mark of patristic exegesis."[30]

Let's follow McGuckin's lead and ponder comments from Cyril of Alexandria on "Jesus Christ." In one passage from Cyril's *Homilies on the Gospel of Luke*, he emphasizes that many of the words, events, and actions of Jesus' life were predicted by Old Testament prophets. For example, as Jesus and the disciples share table fellowship after his resurrection, Jesus' goal is to help them understand why he had to die in such a horrific fashion, and to empower them for the ministry he is now preparing them to undertake under the guidance and empowerment of the Holy Spirit.

So much had happened! What did it all mean? Jesus "quieted" the apostles' "reasonings by what he said, by the touch of their hands, and by eating the food..."[31] As they ate together, "he then opened their mind to understand that it was necessary for him to suffer, even on the wood of the cross."[32]

Jesus focuses the disciples' minds on teaching he had previously given them, "for he had forewarned them of his sufferings on the cross, according to what the prophets had spoken long before, and he opens also the eyes of their heart, for them to understand the ancient prophecies."[33] The apostles need both understanding and empowerment.

As Jesus teaches them, he "recalls the minds of the disciples to what he had said beforehand, for he had forewarned them of his sufferings on the cross, according to what the prophets had spoken long before, *and he also*

---

30. Ibid.
31. Cyril of Alexandria, *Homilies on the Gospel of Luke* 24.45; ACD 2.12. I have slightly modified the translation.
32. Ibid.
33. Ibid.

opens the eyes of their heart, for them to understand the ancient prophecies."[34] The disciples must preach with knowledge and power.

The Holy Spirit, in fulfillment of Joel's prophecy (*Joel* 2:28), will baptize them. "The Savior promises the disciples the descent of the Holy Spirit that God had announced by Joel, and power from above, that they might be strong and invincible and preach to all, everywhere, without any fear, the divine mystery."[35]

The disciples receive the Spirit as Jesus breathes on them and are instructed to remain in Jerusalem to "wait for the promise of the Father, of which you have heard from me. For John indeed baptized with water, but you shall be baptized with the Holy Spirit" (*Acts* 1:5). With the fulfillment that occurs in Acts 1, Jesus ascends to heaven. Cyril comments: "Having blessed them and gone a little in advance, he was carried even to heaven, that he might share the Father's throne even with the flesh that was united to him."[36]

Cyril clearly teaches that the incarnate Word -- Jesus Christ -- has prepared a "new pathway . . . for us when he appeared in human form."[37] The ascension, though, is not the end of the story. For "in due time he will come again in the glory of his Father with the angels and will take us up to be with him."[38]

How should we respond to the Word, now incarnate as Jesus Christ? We worship and glorify him. "Therefore, let us glorify him who, being God the Word, became man for our sakes; who suffered willingly in the flesh, and rose from the dead, and abolished corruption; who was taken up, and hereafter shall come with great glory to judge the living and the dead and will give to each according to their deeds; by whom and with whom to God the Father be glory and power with the Spirit, to ages of the ages. Amen."[39]

This last quotation, a doxology, sums up well what the African church fathers understood "Jesus Christ" to mean:

---

34. Ibid; my emphasis.
35. Ibid.
36. Ibid.
37. Ibid.
38. Ibid, ACD 2.12-13.
39. Ibid, ACD 2.13.

- He is the pre-existent divine *logos,* God the Word.
- God the Word became a man, a male human being, for our sakes.
- He suffered willingly in his body.
- He rose from the dead.
- He abolished corruption.
- He ascended into heaven.
- He shall return in glory to judge the living and the dead.
- He will give to each person according to their deeds.

This summary illustrates well the North African perspective on Jesus Christ. Do you see how Cyril emphasizes key aspects of the Nicene Creed, which had been composed when he was around five years old?

When we consult Clement of Alexandria, who was born in Athens, Greece, and moved to Alexandria around 180 CE, we encounter many comments that reflect an early understanding concerning Jesus Christ that are similar to Cyril's. He is the "Word," the divine *logos,* "who was in God . . . and has now himself appeared to humankind." Jesus "alone is both God and man". He is the Word "who was in the beginning and who was before the beginning. And now, quite recently, he has been manifested, the Savior who was before. . . But now, when we were perishing, he has appeared and saved us."[40]

"THE ONLY SON OF GOD"

The Nicene Creed proceeds to state that the "one Lord, Jesus Christ," is *"the only Son of God,"* our next phrase to explore. John McGuckin captures well the importance of these words. "The Nicene fathers were to insist, as they sought for a calm center in the storm of controversy, that the church's confession of Jesus as the only Son of God expressed clearly enough that the Lord was not one of many saints or angelic powers who could be designated by such a name. He was what the church had sensed from the beginning: Son of God in a unique sense."[41]

We now are going to return to Arius, and more fully explore why he

---

40. Clement of Alexandria, *Exhortation to the Greeks* 1.7; ACD 2.14.
41. ACD 2.24.

struggled with believing that Jesus could be God. His difficulties with this idea are not only related to his thoughts on the incarnation. It's fair to say they are related more deeply to the nature of God and what the church came to formulate as the doctrine of the Holy Trinity.

Here is the problem in a nutshell, one that all Christians faced in the fourth century CE: How can God be one and three? How can the Son be God? How can the Spirit be God? How can they be God, if the Father is God?

These questions are related to a truth that all the church fathers affirmed: God is simple. What does God's simplicity mean? God is not a composite being. If God is simple, God is indivisible, noncomposite. God can't be divided up into parts, or persons. If so, Arius reasoned, can genuine relational distinctions within the being of God be possible?

Arius's belief in God's simplicity – which the entire church affirmed -- appeared to him to be a roadblock to Jesus' divinity, for if he was divine God must be composite – the Father, Son, and Holy Spirit.

Things erupted in Alexandria, Arius's hometown, when Alexander – Arius's bishop – began to teach very clearly about Jesus' divinity and its implication for relations between the Father, Son, and Holy Spirit. Here's what Alexander was teaching – and rightly so: "Always Father, always Son." "Father and Son together." "The eternal begotten." "Neither in thought nor by a single instant is God before the Son." "Always God, always Son." "The Son is of God himself."[42]

Arius responded to Alexander with a firm "No." This relational complexity within the being of God was absolutely impossible. Why? God is simple, indivisible, and cannot generate another Son who is also God. To be God is to be "ingenerate," "unbegotten," "unalterable," and "unchangeable." "We acknowledge one God, Who is alone Ingenerate, alone Everlasting, alone Unbegotten, alone True, alone having Immortality, alone Wise, alone Good, alone Sovereign; Judge, Governor, and Providence of all, unalterable and unchangeable, just and good, God of Law and Prophets and New Testament."[43]

Arius and his followers refused to affirm that the Son is equal to the

---

42. Arius, *The Letter of Arius to Eusebius of Nicomedia* in *Christology of the Later Fathers*, by Edward R. Hardy, (Philadelphia: Westminster Press, 1954), 330. Cf. JND Kelly, *Early Christian Creeds* (London: Longmans, Green, and Co., 1950), 232.
43. Arius is quoted by Athanasius in his *De Synodis* 16, NPNF 2:458.

Father. Can you see why? Relational complexity within God was not possible, for God was simple, not made up of parts or persons. God could not timelessly generate a Son who was equal to God.[44] God's own being as simple – not composite -- made this impossible.

To be fair, Arius's reading of the Bible seemed to be confirmed by key biblical texts. How could Jesus increase "in wisdom and in stature and in favor with God and man" (*Lk* 2:52), if he were equal or "consubstantial" with the Father? God grows in wisdom? God grows in stature?

Carefully consider another of Arius's objections: if God's essence must in some way be divided between Father and Son, God can't be simple; he must be composite in some fashion, an idea both Arius and orthodox church fathers rejected.

So, in response to the teaching of Alexander, Arius proposed an understanding of God that made the Son's divinity impossible. Arius spoke of the Son as "begotten", but not in a sense that Alexander or Athanasius would approve. The Son is "begotten" as an elevated creature, exalted above all other creatures, with a beginning "before times and ages."[45] "And before he was begotten or created or ordained or founded, *he was not*. For he was not unbegotten. We are persecuted because we say, 'The Son has a beginning, but God is without beginning.'"[46]

The storm that raged around the meaning of Jesus for many years centered on who he was. Was he God? Or was he a holy man similar to many of the holy people who had lived in the history of Israel and the church? Perhaps God had adopted him as his Son because of the holiness and devotion of his life? If he was divine, might he be some kind of second-level divine being, perhaps an angel of some kind? Or was Jesus divine in exactly the same way as the God of Israel, so that attributes we would proclaim of God we may rightfully predicate of Jesus?

The answer the church fathers gave to these questions was clear, firm, and direct. Jesus was the incarnate Son of God. At one time, it seemed that only Athanasius, the controversial and courageous African archbishop of

---

44. Readers interested in a more technical discussion of these issues should consult my essay, "The Nicene Creed: Foundation of Orthodoxy," found in Matthew Barrett, Ed., *On Classical Trinitarianism: Retrieving the Nicene Doctrine of the Triune God* (Downers Grove: IVP Academic, 2024), 21-37.
45. Arius, *The Letter of Arius to Eusebius of Nicomedia*, op. cit., 330-331.
46. Ibid; my emphasis.

Alexandria, understood this. The point that Athanasius faithfully reiterated throughout his lifetime was this: Jesus would never have been worshiped by Christians, from the first century onwards, unless he was God. It would have been blasphemous to do so. This is the key starting point for Athanasius.

Once this fundamental truth had been established, the questions facing an African theologian like Athanasius were immense and numerous. How could a human being be God? How could the church simultaneously affirm Jesus' deity and humanity, an assertion that seemed to entail a logical contradiction? What language, what words, what phrases would best preserve and protect the high and holy mystery of the Trinity and the incarnation?

Athanasius is clear and consistent in his great work *Against the Arians*. Recall that the central assertion of the Arian position was that Jesus was the highest and holiest creature that God the Father ever created, but not God. For God was ingenerate. God could not generate a Son because of God's simplicity.

Athanasius realized that if Christ were not God, the gospel was threatened; indeed, it was undercut. Why? One creature cannot save another from the ravages and corruption of sin. Only God can save. The great surprise and wonder was that God had chosen to do so by becoming a creature, a male human being, while simultaneously remaining God.

In response to Arian teaching, Athanasius writes that "He would not have been worshiped or spoken of in this way if he belonged merely to the rank of creatures. But as it is, since he is not a creature but the offspring of the God who is worshiped, an offspring proper to his substance and a Son by nature, this is why he is worshiped and is believed to be God, and is Lord of hosts, and has authority, and is All-sovereign, just as the Father is; for he himself says, 'All things that belong to the Father are mine' (cf. *Jn* 16:15). For it is proper to the Son to have all that the Father has and to be such that the Father is beheld in him, and that through him all things were made and that in him the salvation of all is brought about and established."[47]

---

47. Athanasius, *Against the Arians* 2.24; ACD 2.24-25.

GOD'S OFFSPRING?

How is the Son of God, God's "offspring"? And what does the Nicene Creed mean when it speaks of "the only Son of God, eternally begotten from the Father?" Let's investigate.

First, recognize that the Arians are asking the wrong kinds of questions and providing poor answers to the questions they raise: Do not human fathers "beget" children in time? No human son ever existed before his father begat him. And so, if the analogy holds true, the Arians believed that the Father must in some way be prior to the Son to generate him. This analogical fallacy, Athanasius believes, is precisely the source of the Arians' error. Their analysis begins with how things work with humans, with human practices and possibilities, and proceeds to apply how things apply and operate with humans to God analogically.

Are all analogies off-base then? No. If used carefully, analogies help us understand what the church means when it speaks of the eternal Son. For example, Athanasius uses the sun and its rays as a helpful analogy of the Son's relationship to the Father. The Son "issued from the Father like radiance from the sun itself ... For as the sun remains the same, and is not impaired by the rays poured forth from it, so neither does the Father's essence suffer change, though it has the Son as an image of itself."[48]

Athanasius, when he speaks of the Son as God's "offspring", is not speaking like the Arians. "Now if they are discussing *a man*, then they may argue about his word and his son on the human level. But if they are talking of God, man's creator, *they must not think of him on the human level.*"[49]

Pay close attention to what Athanasius is saying, for he is focusing on a fundamental error in how the Arians are thinking, speaking, and writing about God. They think of how humans procreate, how a father begets children, and apply analogically what is true for humans to God and how God begets the Son eternally. It is true that human procreation does occur in space and time. Human fathers are older and separate from their chil-

---

48. Athanasius, *Decr.* 25.2.
49. Athanasius, *Contra Arianos*, 2.34-35; in *The Early Christian Fathers: A Selection from the writings of the Fathers from St. Clement of Rome to St. Athanasius*, edited and translated by Henry Bettenson (New York: Oxford University Press, 1956), 391; my emphasis.

dren. Begetting does involve division and separation. But not, Athanasius teaches, with God.

* * *

Pause and reflect: Don't panic. I know that I've just tossed a huge cake in your face. It seems like I'm asking you to eat it whole. No, I don't expect that, though I'm convinced the flavor of the cake is rich, sweet, and digestible. I think the best path to follow is to slice Athanasius's words into small slices so we can savor them and not develop indigestion. Indeed, it's fair to say that we'll feed on them throughout the *We Believe* series. Let's break down Athanasius's thoughts that we've covered from his book, *Against the Arians*:

- *Creatures must not be worshiped.* It's especially important for nations, tribes, clans, and persons who have a history of idolatry to heed Athanasius's words. In Africa, the danger would be to worship rather than honor the ancestors or to engage them magically. To offer more than honor would surely violate what Athanasius teaches about the sin of worshiping creatures. Of course, cultures may worship other idols. For instance, many Americans worship possessions; the United States is a materialistic, consumer society, though, in recent years an interest in magic and the supernatural is on the rise.
- Athanasius emphasizes his fundamental point. Jesus is not the creature that Arian teaching proposes, because he is worshiped by Christians, *even in Arian churches.* Rather, Jesus is God.
- The question then becomes what kind of language should Christians use in speaking of Jesus as God? What words and phrases best express this mystery? We see Athanasius working these questions in the section I have just quoted from *Against the Arians.*
- Jesus doesn't belong "merely" to the "rank of creatures." He is more than a human being. He is "the offspring of the God who is worshiped." God the Father has a Son, who has become incarnate in "Jesus Christ." Remember, Jesus is a wondrous beauty, a divine gift and saving surprise for the entire world. It

was not thought possible that God could become a human being, yet this is exactly what has happened.
- Because the Son is divine by "substance" and by "nature," he is worthy of our worship. Not only should the incarnate Son be worshiped, but what we predicate of the Father we can and should predicate of the Son. Why? Because the incarnate Son is God. Athanasius makes this clear when he calls Jesus the "Lord of hosts."
- Carefully ponder the titles and characteristics Athanasius applies to Jesus, the Son of God. It really is quite astounding. He is "Lord of hosts." He has "authority." He is "All-sovereign, just as the Father is."
- Is this biblical teaching? Of course it is. Athanasius turns our attention to the gospel of John. "All things that belong to the Father are mine" (Jn 16:15). "Lord, show us the Father, and we will be satisfied" (Jn 14:8). Jesus seems frustrated with Philip and the other disciples. "Have I been with you all this time Philip, and you still do not know me? Whoever has seen me has seen the Father. How can you say to me, 'Show us the Father?" (Jn 14:9).
- Since Jesus is God, it is correct to say, "that through him all things were made and that in him the salvation of all is brought about and is established." Yes, indeed, for only God can save.[50]

FURTHER HELP FROM CYRIL OF ALEXANDRIA AND AUGUSTINE

* * *

Pause and reflect: Let's pause for a moment and shift from Athanasius back to Cyril of Alexandria and Augustine. They both meditated deeply on John 14:10 and its implications for the relationship between the Father, the Son, and the Holy Spirit. First carefully read Jesus' words: "Do you not believe that I am in the Father and the Father is in me? The words

---

50. Athanasius, *Against the Arians* 2.24; ACD 2.25.

that I say to you I do not speak on my own; but the Father who dwells in me does his works"(14:10). Before continuing, try to formulate three phrases that express the implications of John 14:10 for Jesus's deity.

* * *

Cyril comments that John's text clearly presents the equality between the Father and the Son. Indeed, "so great is the equality in essence between myself [Jesus] and him that my words are his words, and whatever I do may be believed to be his actions . . . For since the Godhead is one in the Father, in the Son, and in the Spirit, every word that comes from the Father comes through the Son by the Spirit. Every work or miracle is through the Son by the Spirit, and yet it is considered as coming from the Father. For the Son is not apart from the essence of the Father, nor indeed is the Holy Spirit. But the Son, being in the Father and having the Father again in himself, claims that the Father is the doer of the works. For the nature of the Father is mighty in operation and shines out clearly in the Son."[51]

* * *

Pause and reflect: There are many truths in Cyril's words to ponder. Take time to prayerfully contemplate each one. We don't want to rush through Cyril's thoughts. They are rich and deep:

- The Father's words are the Son's words. The Father and Son speak with one voice. *It is impossible for them to disagree. They will never enter into an argument with each other*, i.e. "I think we should do this," says the Father. "No, I think we should do that," says the Son. No, no. The Father and Son share the same "essence", the same "being." And the essence they share as different "persons" within the Trinity is the essence of God.
- How can the Father's words also be those of the Son? They are one God. They are equal in essence. ". . . so great is the equality

---

51. Cyril, *Commentary on the Gospel of John* 9; ACCS 14b.132.

in essence shared between them... every word that comes from the Father comes through the Son by the Holy Spirit."
- What should we conclude? Everything we predicate of God, we proclaim as true of the Father. Everything we predicate of God, we proclaim as true of the Son. Everything we predicate of God, we proclaim as true of the Holy Spirit. Does the Father know all things? Yes. And so does the Son. And so does the Holy Spirit. The only difference between the persons of the Trinity is relational in character.
- The Father's actions are the Son's actions through the Holy Spirit.
- The essence of God is "shared" by all three persons of the Holy Trinity.

Cyril's thoughts are very rich; we must chew on them slowly so that we don't get indigestion! As we chew, their nutrients will flow into our spiritual blood stream. Write down three of Cyril's comments that were new understandings for you.

AUGUSTINE ON JOHN 14:10

Now let's explore the thought of Augustine on the same verse from John's gospel: "Don't you believe that I am in the Father, and that the Father is in me? The words I say to you I do not speak on my own authority. Rather, it is the Father living in me, who is doing his work."

Augustine then writes: "The Father was not born of the Virgin, and yet this birth of the Son from the Virgin was the work of both the Father and Son. The Father did not suffer on the cross, and yet the passion of the Son was the work of both the Father and the Son. The Father did not rise again from the dead, and yet the resurrection of the Son was the work of both Father and Son. You have the persons quite distinct, and their working inseparable. So let us never say that the Father worked anything without the Son, the Son anything without the Father."[52]

* * *

---

52. Augustine, *Sermon* 52.14; ACCS 4b.132.

Pause and reflect: I suggest memorizing this line from Augustine: *"You have the persons quite distinct, and their working inseparable."* We must always preserve the relational distinctions between the persons, while simultaneously affirming that we are referring to the one, true God.

* * *

Augustine emphasizes that the actions of the Trinity -- the Father, Son, and Holy Spirit -- are *inseparable*. "So, then, with all these ways of speaking we still have to understand that the activities of the divine three are inseparable, so that when an activity is attributed to the Father he is not taken to engage in it without the Son and Holy Spirit. And when it is an activity of the Son, it is not without the Father and the Holy Spirit. And when it is an activity of the Spirit, it is not without the Father and the Son."[53]

We've covered significant ground. We now understand that the works of the Holy Trinity are one; the works of the Father, Son, and Holy Spirit are inseparable, because God is one. As Christians, we worship one God, not three. The African fathers expressed this very clearly.

It is the Son who becomes incarnate for the sake of the world, not the Father, though the Father, Son, and Holy Spirit are in full agreement that the incarnation must take place and work together to accomplish this wonder. It is impossible for them to disagree about anything.

". . . ETERNALLY BEGOTTEN OF THE FATHER"

The next statement of the Nicene Creed declares that the Son of God is "eternally begotten of the Father." As we've seen, the language of the Father begetting the Son is strange at first glance. What does it mean? And not mean?

The divine begetting is not like human begetting. Rather, the Son is *eternally* begotten by the Father. There was never a "time" when this begetting began. It is eternal in nature. The Son is "eternally begotten of the Father," a begetting outside of time, and of course, apart from bodies, for God is not embodied. God is Spirit (cf. *Jn* 4:24).

---

53. Augustine, *Sermon* 71.26; ACCS 4b.133.

The Creed declares the very thing Arius taught was impossible. Arius argued that God could not have an eternal Son and still be one God, a unity. To Arius's mind, the language of "unbegotten" and "begotten" necessitated at least two gods, a horrible idea to him if one believed in only one God. Thus, Arius taught that the Son was an elevated creature with a beginning in time.

To Arius's mind, the idea of eternal personal relations within the being of God made no sense. God was one. Accordingly, there was a time when the Son did not exist. In Arius's language, there was a time "when he was not."

No, the Creed states. "The Son is eternally begotten of the Father." The Father has *always* begotten the Son. The Son is the "only begotten" from eternity. His begetting by the Father has no beginning and no end. It always "is."

Remember Origen's words: ". . . nothing can be found in existence or conceived or imagined that can compare with God."[54] For God is incomparable. God is utterly unique. "Human thought cannot apprehend how the unbegotten God becomes the Father of the only-begotten Son." Why? "For it is an eternal and ceaseless generation, as radiance is generated from Light."[55]

This is an extremely important point. Origen's analogy of the sun and its rays is helpful. The sun cannot exist apart from its radiance. To be the sun is by definition to emit light. The light does not start shining after the sun is created. Origen gets this just right. Similarly, the Son's generation "is an eternal generation, as radiance is generated from light. . . He is the radiance of the eternal light, the unblemished mirror of the activity of God and the image of his goodness (cf. *Col* 1:15; *Heb* 1:3) . . . he alone is Son by nature; and this is why he is called Only-Begotten."[56]

Origen helps us fine tune our understanding. "The existence of the Son is generated by the Father."[57] This is an eternal generation. The Son derives his eternal existence from the Father, not the Father from the Son. *For only the Father is underived or unbegotten.*

Have you noticed that there is a clear order or *taxis* (Gk.) within the

---

54. Origen, *On First Principles*, 1.2.4-5: ACD 2.33.
55. Ibid.
56. Ibid.
57. Origen, *On First Principles*, 1.2.6; ACD 2.33.

Trinity? The Father is unbegotten. The Son is eternally begotten from the Father. This relation can never be reversed, for to be Father is to be unbegotten, and to be Son is to be eternally begotten of the Father.

Phillip Cary's thoughts are very helpful. When the Nicene Creed speaks of the Son as "eternally begotten of the Father," Cary comments that "we find ourselves at the center of the mystery of God. It is language that points paradoxically at what is beyond all language, as it speaks of the origination of the eternal Son of God from his Father. Unlike God the Father, the Son does have an origin: he is 'of the Father,' where 'of' has the sense of 'from,' one thing coming *from* another. The Father is unbegotten, unoriginated ... The Son is different: he does have an origin, for he comes from the Father."[58]

HELP FROM TERTULLIAN

The African Tertullian saw clearly that God's Word, God's *logos,* was always present with the Father. The Word, another name for the Son, has no beginning, for the Word is eternal. Think of John 1:1. "In the beginning was the Word, and the Word was with God, and the Word was God." Tertullian explains: "Before all things existed, God was alone. He was himself his own universe, his own place, everything. He was alone in the sense that there was nothing external to him, nothing outside his own being. *Yet even then he was not alone*, for he had with him something that was part of his own being, namely, his Reason [his Word or *logos*]."[59] This must be the case, Tertullian argues, on the basis of the biblical testimony and on logical principles. "For God is rational, and Reason existed first with him, and from him extended to all things." What is God's reason? The *logos* is God's "own consciousness of himself."[60]

The Greeks named the *logos* God's "discourse." Tertullian, though, explains that "it would be more correct to regard Reason as anterior to Discourse, because there was not Discourse with God from the beginning, but there was Reason, even before the beginning, and because Discourse takes its origin from Reason and thus shows Reason to be prior to it, as

---

58. Phillip Cary, *The Nicene Creed: An Introduction* (Bellingham: Lexham Press, 2023), 59.
59. Tertullian, *Against Praxeas* 5; ACD 2.34.
60. Ibid.

the ground of its being."[61] Still, Tertullian admits, this distinction is really not necessary. "... there is no real difference. Although God has not yet uttered his Discourse, he had it in his own being, and with and in his Reason, and he silently pondered and arranged in his thought those things that he was soon to say by his Discourse.[62]

The wonder and the mystery are that God's reason and discourse are eternal, outside of time. Because God's thought is timeless, it does not proceed in a discursive manner from thought to thought. In a manner of speaking, God's thought is one great thought expressed through his Word, his divine Son.

* * *

Pause and reflect: Ponder your relationship to God. You have always been part of God's one great, eternal thought. That's an encouraging thought, isn't it? There has never been a time when God has not been thinking of you, for it would be impossible for God not to do so! Take a moment and write three implications of this truth for your life.

* * *

BACK TO ATHANASIUS

Athanasius has so much to offer us. I hope that in years to come you spend significant time with him. His thoughts are always worth our time and reflection. Athanasius was the church father who most clearly perceived the error of Arius. To say that God's preincarnate Son was a creature had implications that Arius and his followers simply didn't perceive. We've already seen that Athanasius clearly understood that only God can save from sin, an aspect of his thought we'll return to throughout the *We Believe* series.

What other truths did the Arian perspective misconstrue? Athanasius lists quite a few: "Was God 'who is', ever without his reason? Was he, 'who is light,' without radiance? Or was he always the Father of the Word? . . .

---

61. Ibid.
62. Ibid.

Who can endure to hear them say that God was ever without reason . . . or that God was not always Father?"[63] No. Absolutely not. "God is, eternally." What can we conclude? "Thus, since the Father always is, his brightness exists eternally, and that is his Word. Again, God 'who is' has, derived from himself, the Word who also 'is.'"[64]

In a helpful footnote to Athanasius's text, John McGuckin explains that "Divine existence is self-existence and is to be referred to only in the continuous present, resisting the past or future tenses as inappropriate. 'He who is' is the quintessential divine name as revealed to Moses at the epiphany of the burning bush."[65]

God was not once the Father, but no longer. Nor will God become the Father at some point in the future. No. God is the Father and will always be such. Hence, God is eternally the Father of the Son, who is eternally the Son of the Father. The eternal Word – the Son – never entered into existence, for the Son has always existed.

The Father is never without his Son, who is the eternal Word. Again, Athanasius uses the sun and its rays as a helpful analogy. "If a person looked at the sun and asked, concerning its radiance, 'Did that which is, make something that did not exist before, or something that already existed?', he would not be regarded as reasoning sensibly; he would in fact be crazy in supposing that what comes from the light is something external to it and asking when and where and whether it was made. Such reasoning and such questions about the Son and the Father would display a greater degree of insanity, for this is to make the Word an external addition to the Father and to speak erroneously of a natural offspring as created by saying, 'He did not exist before he was begotten.'"[66] Athanasius teaches as clearly and consistently as he can, the Son is eternally begotten of the Father!

The Father exists eternally as the Father of the Son. Remember, too, that another name for the eternal Word (Jn 1:1) is Jesus as the Wisdom of God. Origen comments: "How could anyone believe that God the Father could have existed at any time without begetting Wisdom . . . for that would be to say either that God could not beget Wisdom before he did

---

63. Athanasius, *Against the Arians* 1.24-25; ACD 2.34.
64. ACD 2.34, footnote 46.
65. Ibid.
66. Ibid.

beget it ... or that he could have done so but did not wish to ... and either supposition is patently absurd and impious. We must believe that Wisdom is without beginning ... He is called the Word because he is, as it were, the interpreter of the secrets of the mind of God."[67]

* * *

Pause and reflect: Consider memorizing the following italicized sentence: *An eternal Father demands the existence of an eternal Son.* As Origen puts it, "The existence of the Son derives from the Father, but not in time, nor does it have any beginning, except in the sense that it starts from God."[68]

* * *

Are you following the argument of these African fathers? It is subtle, sophisticated, and takes some time to absorb. I think Athanasius explains things helpfully and clearly. He asks us to carefully ponder the word "Father." "The Son is implied with the Father, for one cannot use the title 'father' unless a son exists ... in calling God 'Father' we at once intimate the Son's existence. Therefore whoever believes in the Son believes in the Father. . . And whoever worships and honors the Son worships and honors the Father, for the Godhead is one; and therefore there is one honor and one worship that is given to the Father in and through the Son. And one who worships thus worships the one God."[69]

Let's sum up what we have covered thus far before proceeding to the next phrase of the Nicene Creed:

- God is one. Christians worship one God, just like the Jews.
- Yet within the one God there is unexpected relational complexity, a complexity Jesus taught about and demonstrated in addressing God as his Father.
- If God is eternally Father, then he must have an eternal Son.

---

67. Origen, *On First Principles* 1.2.1-3; ACD 2.37.
68. Ibid., 1.2.10; ACD 2.37.
69. Athanasius, *Against the Arians* 3.6; ACD 2.38.

- The eternal Son is not a creature, though the incarnate Jesus is fully human. While existing as a human male, Jesus is simultaneously fully God. With the eternal Son's movement into history with his birth at Bethlehem, something new and unique has occurred. Jesus is the God-Man, fully divine and fully human.
- The Son did not begin to be the Son, for he is eternally the Son of the Father. He did not begin to be the Son at any point in time or outside of time.

"GOD FROM GOD"

Let's explore the next three words of the Nicene Creed, "God from God." If the Son is eternally in relationship with the Father, eternally begotten of the Father, he is "God from God."

At first glance "God from God" seems impossible, especially when we affirm that there is only one God. Yet when we recall the relational complexity within God, "God from God" makes greater sense. This phrase especially emphasizes that when we think of the Son we are not thinking of a creature, as Arius and his supporters had argued. No, the Son is God as the Father is God and is generated timelessly by the Father.

Tertullian comments with helpful analogies we have come to know in this book. God produces his Word (Jn 1:1) "as a root produces the shoot, a spring the river, the sun a ray . . . I would not hesitate to call a shoot 'the son of a root,' a river 'the son of a spring,' a ray 'a son of the sun.' For every original source is a parent. Much more is this true of the Word of God, who has received the name of Son as his proper designation . . . [70]

In all of Tertullian's analogies, the point remains the same. Although a root can be distinguished from its shoot, a spring from its river, and a ray from the sun, they are still one, *though there is a clear order of derivation.*

The Son can be relationally distinguished from the Father, yet they are one God and share the same essence. The Son is "God from God." Once again Athanasius is helpful. As we've seen, the Arians promoted the idea that the Son "is a creature, but not as one of the creatures; a work, but not

---

70. Tertullian, *Against Praxeas* 8; ACD 2.44.

as one of the works; an offspring, but not as one of the offsprings."[71] Athanasius will have none of this "disingenuous talk." If the Son is a creature, he cannot be God.

Athanasius calls us to acknowledge that the Son is God *by nature*. He is not an elevated creature, however high the elevation might be. "But if the whole earth sings the praises of the Creator and the truth, and blesses him and trembles before him, and if its Creator is the Word and he himself says, 'I am the truth' (*Jn* 14:6), then it follows that the Word is not a creature but is the sole true Word of the Father. In him all things are set in order, and he himself has his praises sung by all, as Creator. For he himself says, 'I was at his side, ordering' (*Prov* 8:30), and also 'My Father works until now, and I work" (*Jn* 5:17).[72]

THE IMPORTANCE OF JOHN 5

Athanasius's refers to John 5:17 in his response to the Arians. Always remember the significance of John 5. In this text Jesus lists a number of things God does and then says *he does them in the same way.*

The Father works on the Sabbath and so does Jesus (*Jn* 5:17). Jesus called God his own Father, "making himself equal with God" (*Jn* 5:18). Jesus does what he sees his Father doing, "because whatever the Father does the Son also does" (*Jn* 5:19). Just as the Father raises the dead and "gives them life, even so the Son gives life to whom he is pleased to give it" (*Jn* 5:21).

The Father has given all judgment into the hands of the Son. Why? The Son is *God from God*, as the Nicene Creed proclaims. Jesus calls his listeners "to honor the Son just as they honor the Father. Whoever does not honor the Son does not honor the Father, who sent him" (*Jn* 5:23).

Jesus unapologetically states that just as the Father is the source of life, so is Son. "Just as the Father has life in himself, so he has granted the Son to have life in himself" (*Jn* 5:26). Finally, Jesus tops things off by declaring that "a time is coming when all who are in their graves will hear his voice and come out – those who have done what is good will rise to live, and those who have done what is evil will rise to be condemned" (*Jn* 5:28-29).

---

71. Athanasius, *Against the Arians* 2.19-20; ACD 2.45
72. Ibid.

African church fathers read John 5 and correctly concluded that the incarnate Jesus was "God from God." What other conclusion could they reach, as difficult as Jesus' divinity was to comprehend? Athanasius gets it just right. "The character of the parent determines the character of the offspring. People are begotten in time and beget in time; they come into being from nonexistence, and therefore their word ceases and does not remain. But 'God is not like humankind' (*Judith* 8:16), as the Scripture has said; but rather, he is 'he who exists' (*Ex* 3:14) and exists forever. Therefore his Word is 'that which exists' and exists eternally with the Father, as radiance from a light."[73]

The popular patristic analogy between the sun and its rays and the Father and the Son finally breaks down, like all analogies and metaphors do. For the sun did not always exist, and one day it will disappear. Not so with the Father and the Son.

The relationship between the two is eternal, outside the boundaries of time and space. "The whole being of the Son belongs to the Father's substance, *as radiance from light and stream from source.* He who sees the Son sees what belongs to the Father and knows that the Son's being is in the Father just as it is from the Father. For the Father is in the Son *as the sun is in its radiance, the thought in the word, the source in the stream.*"[74]

* * *

Pause and reflect: You might consider collecting all the analogies we have considered thus far in this book and memorize them. The sun and its rays and a river and its source are a good place to begin. Sift the book for other helpful analogies, while always remembering that analogies finally break down. They take us a certain distance, but no farther. As you go on your analogy search, ask yourself what the direction is of the analogy. What is it directing your attention to?

* * *

The Son is "God from God." Though the Son is clearly relationally distinct

---

73. Athanasius, *Against the Arians* 2.34-35; ACD 2.46.
74. Athanasius, *Against the Arians* 3.3-4; ACD 2.46; my emphasis.

from the Father, we must never fall into the error of thinking God is actually two gods, or three gods if we include the Holy Spirit. Athanasius realizes this conceptual error is a real possibility and points to Jesus' teaching in John 10 to remind us that the Father and the Son are "one" (*Jn* 10:30). "I and the Father are one," Jesus teaches, not two.

Yet they are two while remaining one. For they have eternally – outside of time – been relationally distinct and will remain so for all eternity. Some ancient Christians tried to solve this strange Trinitarian arithmetic by teaching that "God" progressively reveals himself in history, first as Father and then as Son. If this were true, the relational distinction between the Father and Son is neither eternal nor essential, but rather a progressive revelation within history as it unfolds. The "Father" and "Son" are simply names that God chooses to use as God reveals himself progressively in the history of Israel and the world. Sabellius advocated this position.

Athanasius's response to Sabellius and those who followed his teaching was a firm "no"! The Father and Son are "one," not "in the sense of one thing with two names, so that the Son is at one time Father, at another time his own Son. Sabellius held this opinion and was condemned as a heretic."[75] The Father and Son are genuinely "two, in that the Father is father and not also son; the Son is son and not also father; but the nature is one (for the offspring is not unlike the parent, being his image), and all that is the Father's is the Son's."[76]

There is no Godhead or source of divinity outside the Father. If there was, we would have two gods, not one. The Son is "distinct" from the Father as his "offspring, even though as God he is identical with him. He and the Father are one by a specific and proper nature and by the identity of the one Godhead."[77]

To reinforce his point Athanasius returns to his favorite analogy or metaphor.

For the radiance also is light, not a second light besides the sun, or a different light or a light by participation in the sun, but a whole proper offspring of it. No one would say that there are two lights, even though

---

75. Ibid.
76. Ibid.
77. Ibid.

the sun and its radiance are two. Evidently the light from the sun, which illuminates things everywhere, is one. *In the same way the Godhead of the Son is the Father's.* This is why it is undivided and why 'God is one, and there is none other besides him' (*Isa* 45.5). Accordingly, since they are one, and the Godhead itself is one, the same things are predicated of the Son as of the Father, except the title of 'Father.' So, for instance: 'God' – the Word was God (*Jn* 1:1); 'All sovereign' – 'Thus says he who was and is and is coming, the all-sovereign' (*Rev* 1:8); 'Lord' – 'one Lord, Jesus Christ' (1 *Cor* 8:6); and 'Light' – 'I am the Light' (*Jn* 8:12).[78]

A PARTING WORD FROM AUGUSTINE

I've given you lots to study and ponder. In a sense, we're learning our Trinitarian ABC's. Let's close this chapter with a look at the insights of the great African Augustine as he comments on "God from God."

Augustine realizes that if the Son is one God with the Father, their actions must be one because their will must be one. Thus, the incarnation -- the entrance of the eternal Son into human history as Jesus Christ is the work of God -- the holy Trinity -- including the Holy Spirit. Augustine writes: "There is one will of Father and Son, and one inseparable activity. Thus . . . one may understand that the incarnation and birth from a virgin, by which the Son is understood to have been 'sent,' was effected by one and the same activity of Father and Son, working inseparably and, of course, with the Holy Spirit not separated from the work, as is plainly said: 'She was found pregnant by the Holy Spirit.'"[79]

---

78. Ibid; my emphasis.
79. Augustine, *The Trinity* 2.9; ACD 2.47.

2
LIGHT FROM LIGHT

... Light from Light, True God from True God, Begotten Not Made, of One Being with the Father. Through Him All Things were Made.

Our phrase for this chapter concerns Jesus Christ, the eternal Word now made flesh in the incarnation. Jesus is described as "light from light," "true God from true God," "begotten not made," "of one being with the Father," and as the one through whom "all things were made."

The Nicene Creed emphasizes that when we encounter Jesus, we're encountering God. He is God incarnate, God "with skin on," as a friend likes to say. Let's begin our exploration of Christ's glory with a closer look at the first phrase, "Light from Light."

"LIGHT FROM LIGHT"

It is significant, indeed amazing, how often light and God are linked in the Bible. Almost an entire page in *The NIV Complete Concordance* is devoted to light and God, light and God's actions in the history of Israel, and light and the saving acts of God in Christ. For our purposes here, let's examine key biblical texts to illustrate the Nicene Creed's description of Jesus as "light from light."

In the Bible light is often seen when the glory of God is manifested at a geographical location or through a particular person. After Moses receives the tablets of stone from God on Mount Sinai his face shines; it is radiant. He has been in the presence of God and witnessed his glory. "When Moses came down from Mount Sinai with the two tablets of the covenant law in his hands, he was not aware that his face was radiant because he had spoken with the Lord. When Aaron and all the Israelites saw Moses, his face was radiant, and they were afraid to come near him" (*Ex* 34:29-30, NIV). Because of this radiance, Moses veils his face (*Ex* 34:33, NIV).

Near the beginning of Matthew's gospel, he quotes Isaiah 9:2: "The people living in darkness have seen a great light; on those living in the land of the shadow of death a light has dawned" (*Mt* 4:16). With the arrival of Jesus in human history, darkness is invaded by light. A "light has dawned" over those "living in the land of the shadow of death." When Jesus arrives on the scene, light dawns.

Not only does Jesus bring light, but Jesus *is* light. Jesus as light will be an important theme for the church fathers. Matthew turns our attention to the transfiguration. Jesus leads Peter, James, and John up "a high mountain." "There," Matthew writes, "he was transfigured before them. His face shone like the sun, and his clothes became as white as the light" (*Mt* 17:2).

The North African Origen encourages us to "be attentive spiritually" to Matthew's text. "It is not simply said that he was transfigured, but with a certain addition. Both Matthew and Mark have recorded this: he was transfigured before them."[1] God wanted Peter, James, and John to see Jesus transfigured. Why? They were to be witnesses. And what they witnessed was the glory of God shining through Jesus.

As Origen describes the scene, what these three apostles saw was twofold. They saw Jesus "according to the flesh." That is, they looked at Jesus and saw a human being. But the human being they saw was beaming with light. They beheld, in Origen's words, "his true divinity."[2]

Simultaneously, the disciples see both aspects of who Jesus is. "He is beheld in the form of God according to our capacity for knowledge."[3] Jesus is purposely expanding the disciples' vision and knowledge of who

---

1. Origen, *Commentary on Matthew* 12.37; *Ancient Christian Commentary on Scripture* (ACCS), NT 1b, Matthew 14-28, edited by Manlio Simonetti (Downers Grove: InterVarsity Press, 2002), 53.
2. Ibid.
3. Ibid.

he is. Jesus desires for the apostles to know him in his fullness, and he wants us to see the same thing. Though human, he is also divine. Though he possesses a human body, light – divine light – beams from it. Jesus is luminous with divine glory.

The disciples must learn to embed two marvelous truths in their minds and hearts when they look at Jesus. He is human and he is divine. We see the lasting effect of this truth on the apostle John when we read in his gospel, "The true light that gives light to everyone was coming into the world" (*Jn* 1:9).

Augustine discerns the link between John's experience on the Mount of Transfiguration and what John later writes in his gospel. "Indeed, Jesus himself shone as the sun, indicating that he is the light which illuminates everyone who comes into this world (*Jn* 1:9)."[4]

Note, too, that the two greatest prophets from the Old Testament – Moses and Elijah – are present on the mountain talking with Jesus. Yet God the Father directs the attention of the apostles to Jesus. "This is my Son, whom I love; with him I am well pleased. Listen to him!" (*Mt* 17:5) Augustine comments: "Moses was there, and Elijah. The voice did not say: These are my beloved sons. For One only is the Son; others are adopted. It is he that is commended to them: He from whom the law and prophets derive their glory."[5] Moses and Elijah are invited to be with Jesus as he reveals his identity as God incarnate to Peter, James, and John, for they had helped to prepare his way.

Pause and reflect: In your mind's eye, picture yourself on the Mount of Transfiguration with Jesus and the apostles. At one moment you are simply hiking, climbing the mountain trail with Jesus. Then Jesus stops climbing. In an instant, Moses and Elijah appear and Jesus starts glowing. What does Jesus look like? Try to describe what you are seeing. What does the Father want you to see? To hear? Jot down any insights that come.

---

4. Augustine, *Sermon* 78.2; ACCS NT: 1b.54.
5. Augustine, *Sermons on New Testament Lessons*; *Ancient Christian Commentary on Scripture* (ACCS), New Testament, Mark, edited by Thomas C. Oden and Christopher A. Hall (Downers Grove: InterVarsity Press, 1998), 120.

* * *

Cyril of Alexandria comments that

> the law of Moses and the word of the holy prophets foreshadowed the mystery of Christ. The law of Moses foreshadowed it by types and shadows, painting it as in a picture. The holy prophets in different ways declared beforehand that in due time he would appear in our likeness and for the salvation and life of us all. . .It excellently displayed our Lord Jesus Christ as having the law and the prophets for his bodyguard. It displayed Christ as being the Lord of the Law and the Prophets, as foretold in them by those things that they proclaimed in mutual agreement beforehand.[6]

The implications of Cyril's words are important. If Christ is "the Lord of the Law and the Prophets," he is greater than the Law and the Prophets. For he is God incarnate. The light beaming from his body demonstrates this, for "God is light. In him there is no darkness at all" (1 *Jn* 1:5).

John McGuckin summarizes the Nicene Creed's words about Jesus as "light": "When the creed refers to the Son of God as 'Light from Light,' therefore, it is specifically annotating the relationship of Son to Father and describing it in biblical terms as the single Glory of God shining in the person and the saving work of the Son."[7]

AFRICAN PERSPECTIVES ON "LIGHT FROM LIGHT"

Let's take a closer look at the African church fathers thoughts on the wonderful theme of "Light from Light."

Clement of Alexandria observes the searching power of God's revealing light. Nothing escapes its notice. "As the sun illumines not only the heaven and the whole world, shining on both land and sea, but also sends his rays through windows and small chinks into the furthest

---

6. Cyril of Alexandria, *Commentary on Luke*, Homily 51; *Ancient Christian Commentary on Scripture* (ACCS), New Testament III, Luke, edited by Arthur A. Just, Jr. (Downers Grove: InterVarsity Press, 2003), 159.
7. John McGuckin, ACD 2.49.

recesses of a house, so the Word, poured out everywhere, *beholds the smallest actions of our life.*"[8]

Origen ponders the letter to the Hebrews and its teaching that Christ is "the radiance of God's splendor and the exact representation of his being" (*Heb* 1:3) and couples this insight to John's comment that "God is light" (1 *Jn* 1:5). "The radiance of this light is the only-begotten Son, who proceeds from the Father without separation, as radiance from the light, and gives light to the whole creation."[9]

God accommodates his brightness to us, for we are easily overwhelmed, and slowly unveils its brilliance. "This radiance presents itself gently to the feeble eyes of mortals and gradually trains and accustoms them, as it were, to endure the full blaze of the light."[10]

So we see that God's light is present in the incarnate Jesus. As we've observed in the transfiguration, light beams from Jesus, *as he and his Father allow it to do so.* As Origen discerns, God realizes his uncreated light would easily overwhelm us. As we train our eyes to accustom themselves to God's light by getting to know Jesus better and better, our vision expands, clarifies, and strengthens.

* * *

Pause and reflect: Clement pictures God's revealing light shining "through windows and small chinks into the furthest recesses of a house. . ." Open the windows of your heart and mind to Christ's brilliant light. Do the windows need to be cleaned? What might be obscuring Christ's light? Specific thoughts? Certain actions? Problematic habits? What's the state of your house? Sturdy or shaky? Take time to describe the shape of your house, with special emphasis on its windows. What needs to be repaired? What needs to be cleaned? What needs to be polished?

* * *

---

8. Clement of Alexandria, *Stromateis* 7.3.21; ACD 2.50; my emphasis.
9. Origen, *On First Principles* 1.2.7; ACD 2.50.
10. Ibid.

AN ETERNAL RELATIONSHIP

The relationship between the Father and the Son is eternal. It has no beginning, continues unabated after the incarnation, and will have no end. To know the Son is to know the eternal Father. To see the Son is to see the eternal Father. To worship the Son is to worship the eternal Father. The relationship between the Father and Son is eternal. It has always existed. Always. It never began. It will never end.

As Athanasius understands clearly, God's light is necessarily accompanied by its radiance. Indeed, radiance finds its source in light. "We see that the radiance from the sun is integral to it and that the substance of the sun is not divided or diminished, but its substance is entire, and its radiance perfect and entire, and the radiance does not diminish the substance of the light, but is as it were a genuine offspring from it."[11] This popular patristic analogy illustrates well the relationship between the Father and the Son, yet like all analogies if asked to bear too much weight will break. Father and Son share exactly the same essence or substance. Yet the Son finds his source in the Father, much like the radiance of the sun finds its source in the sun itself.

Tuck away in your mind Athanasius's use of "offspring" as illustrative of the Son's relationship with the Father. Light and "offspring" seem to be mixed metaphors, yet Athanasius uses "offspring" quite often when referring to the Son as "begotten" of the Father.

To be the Son is to have a Father. The one demands the existence of the other. If you address God as Father, you implicitly declare your belief in the Son. Clement makes this very point. "Nor does the Father exist without the Son, for 'Father' immediately implies 'Father of a Son,' and the Son is the true teacher about the Father. And in order that a person may believe in the Son, he must know of the Father in relation to the Son."[12]

Not only is the Son of God "true light from true light," but as such he breaks into the darkness of the world. As Origen expresses, "he becomes the light of humankind, when people who had been plunged in darkness

---

11. Athanasius, *Against the Arians* 2.33; ACD 2.50.
12. Clement of Alexandria, *Stromateis* 5.5 (1); ACD 2.52.

by wickedness need 'the light that shines in the darkness and is not overcome by darkness' (Jn 1:5).[13]

When the Son enters our world, he comes in a manner that shields his splendor, and gradually heals our sight. There will come a time when we can gaze upon his glory with eyes that can bear that glorious brilliance. "The Word comes down at a certain time to be with us who cannot behold the splendor and brightness of his Godhead and, as it were, becomes flesh, uttered in bodily terms, until such time as the one who has received him in this shape, being gradually raised to a higher level by the Word, may be able to gaze upon him in his primary form."[14]

Let's sum up the thought of these African church fathers on "light from light":

- Light is often connected with the glory of God in Scripture.
- God's light is sometimes connected with a specific geographical location or significant individual, such as Mt. Sinai or Moses.
- With the arrival of Jesus Christ, "a new light has dawned" in the history of Israel and more broadly in human history.
- The light of Christ will radiate out from Israel to the Gentile world.
- The transfiguration demonstrates both the humanity and divinity of Jesus.
- The appearance of Moses and Elijah with Jesus on the Mount of Transfiguration indicates that Jesus' appearance was in line with the law and the prophetic tradition of Israel.
- Christ is Lord of both the law and the prophets.
- Christ's light is penetrating, illuminating every nook and cranny of our lives.
- The Son is the light of the Father, analogically similar to rays of the sun radiating from its surface.
- The light of the incarnate Son – Jesus of Nazareth – is redemptively penetrating the darkness of this fallen world, and of our own souls.

---

13. Origen, *Commentary on the Gospel of John* 1.20. (22); ACD 2.52.
14. Origen, *Against Celsus* 4.15; ACD 2.52.

PRACTICAL IMPLICATIONS

Before moving on to the next clause in the Nicene Creed, let's explore some practical implications of Jesus as "light from light." Recall that Jesus is the eternal Son of God. As the Son, he has always existed as uncreated light. "God is light and in him there is no darkness at all" (1 Jn 1:5). He will never cease shedding light, for God cannot change. He is "Light from Light."

When the Son entered our world at his birth in Bethlehem, he willingly and gracefully joined his divine nature to the human nature freely offered to him by the Virgin Mary, and Jesus of Nazareth was born. In the wonder and mystery of the incarnation, Jesus never ceased to be God. No change occurred in his divine nature when he entered our world. Yet in the incarnation the divine nature of the Son was joined in an ineffable union to human nature.

In Jesus' person and ministry, his uncreated light as God occasionally manifests itself. Think of the Transfiguration. Luke describes the scene. "As he was praying, the appearance of his face changed, and his clothes became as bright as a flash of lightning. Two men, Moses and Elijah, appeared in glorious splendor, talking with Jesus. They spoke about his departure, which he was about to bring to fulfillment at Jerusalem (*Lk* 9:29-31, NIV)

Why did Jesus and his Father choose to reveal his radiant glory at this specific time? After all, they manifested his glory in other ways throughout Jesus' ministry. We find the answer in what swiftly happens after the Transfiguration. As Luke writes, Moses, Elijah, and Jesus talk about the "departure" soon to occur in Jerusalem.

Soon the disciples will witness first-hand the horror of Christ's agony in the Garden of Gethsemane, his trial and flogging, the mocking crown of thorns, his long, agonized trek through Jerusalem's streets, burdened by the weight of the cross and the world's sin, and finally the horrific, wicked spectacle of the crucifixion. *By all appearances*, everything has gone wrong. The disciples' hopes have unraveled. Evil seems to have triumphed.

The light beaming from Christ's face and clothing at the Transfiguration served to remind the disciples that the man dying on the cross was identical with the Lord who had manifested his glory to Peter, James and

John. He had not changed. Yet on the cross, Jesus' glory was veiled. For three days, his glory is hidden, but *never ceased shining*.

Yes, in his humanity the Son died; his human soul separated from his body. But his divine light continued to shine, though veiled from those gazing on the cross. Sadly, the horror of those days overcame the disciples, and they failed to remember the glory they had seen at the Transfiguration.

* * *

Pause and reflect: Peter Kreeft, a Christian and philosopher emeritus at Yale University, comments that God is unchangeably faithful. "Fidelity is his unchangeable nature. Everything he promises, he delivers. *Just as the sun can't not give light,* God can't *not* give justice; freedom; sight to the blind; truth to the ignorant; protection to the weak; help to the lonely, the fatherless, and the widow . . . He is our heavenly Father . . . He is love through and through, nothing but love, all-loving love, all-powerful love, and all-knowing love."[15]

How have God's promises and faithfulness manifested themselves in your life? Write down three specific instances where you have experienced God's faithfulness.

When contemplating Jesus as "Light from Light," remember Christ's light is literal light, and also viewed by the church fathers as a metaphor, a symbol of Jesus' unwavering faithfulness and love for you – and me. When by all appearances everything has gone wrong, Christ's light is a promise that everything will turn out right. Can you think of situations in your life where this has proved true? Note down one or two.

* * *

---

15. Peter Kreeft, *Food for the Soul*, Reflections on the Mass Readings, Cycle A (Park Ridge, Il: Word on Fire, 2002), 39; my emphasis.

3
TRUE GOD

True God from True God

*O*ur next clause in the Nicene Creed makes sense in light of the eternal relationship between the Father and the Son. If God's light is shining from God's light, like the radiance of the sun's rays from the sun, the expression "true God from true God" captures well the wonder and beauty of God, the Holy Trinity. What does "true God from true God" indicate? The Son is true God, just as the Father is true God. They share the same divine nature and attributes. The only difference between them is that the Father is not the Son, and the Son is not the Father. They are relationally distinct.

Hence, what we predicate of the Father as God can also be expressed as true of the Son. Origen writes: "He himself is wisdom itself and righteousness itself and truth itself; is he not also sovereignty itself?"[1] And, of course, the answer is yes, for we worship one God, not two gods with separate or different attributes.

Though the Son is sent by the Father to redeem the world in the incarnation, Augustine comments that "this in no way hinders our belief that

---

1. Origen, *Commentary on the Gospel of Matthew* 14.7; ACD 2.54.

the Son is equal to the Father, consubstantial and coeternal, and yet the Son is sent by the Father."[2]

The fact that the Father sends the Son does not mean that the Father is greater than the Son. It indicates, rather, that the Father begets the Son. In Augustine's words, "Not because one is greater than the other, but because one is the Father, the other Son. One is begetter, the other begotten. The Son is from the Father, not the Father from the Son."[3]

Augustine links his discussion with what we've seen previously concerning the Son as "light from light." "For the brightness of light is light and is coeternal with the light from which it springs. If the brightness is less than the light, it is its obscurity, not its brightness."[4]

It is extremely important to understand that all we say of the Father, every divine attribute we predicate of the Father, is also true of the Son. The African fathers stressed this truth, one that kept the church from slipping into ditheism, or the belief in two gods.

Listen carefully to Clement of Alexandria and his description of the Son.

> Most perfect, most holy, most lordly, most commanding, royal and beneficent is the nature of the Son, most closely joined to the Almighty . . . He is always everywhere and not circumscribed anywhere. He is wholly mind, wholly the Father's light, all eye, seeing all things, hearing all things, knowing all things, searching out the powers by his power. The whole army of angels . . . is subject to him. . . .[5]

Athanasius writes that when the Son is born of the Virgin Mary, he becomes fully human, while remaining fully divine. "He calls the Father Lord, not because he was a servant but because he 'took the form of a servant' (*Phil* 2:7). For it was right for him on the one hand to call God 'Father,' as being the Word from the Father; on the other hand, to call the Father 'Lord,' since he came 'to finish the work' (*Jn* 17:4) and took a servant's form."[6]

---

2. Augustine, *The Trinity* 4.27; ACD 2.27.
3. Ibid.
4. Ibid.
5. Clement of Alexandria, *Stromateis* 8.2.5; ACD 2.58.
6. Athanasius, *Against the Arians* 2.50-51; ACD 2.59.

God the Son and God the Father share the same divine essence. They are *homoousios* (Gk.), of the same essence. Yet it is the Son assumes human nature, not the Father. So, we can say things of the incarnate Son that we wouldn't state of the Father. For instance, the incarnate Son has a human nature; the Father does not.

We have to be careful in how we use words. Some things we say about the Son concern the "economy" or "dispensation." Tuck those two words away in your memory bank. When an African writer uses the word "dispensation" or "economy," he is thinking of God's saving work in human history, as the Son becomes incarnate on our behalf to save and to restore.

At other times, the church fathers speak of the "essential" relationship between the Father and the Son, which is by definition eternal. The Son is eternally the Son of the Father, and the Father is eternally the Father of the Son. The Son as Son has no beginning, for he has always been the Son in relation to the Father, eternally generated or begotten by the Father.

IN WHAT WAY IS THE FATHER GREATER THAN THE SON?

This distinction between the "economic" and the "essential" relationship between the Father and Son helps us to understand Jesus' teaching about himself. Probably a few readers have been wondering how we can say the Son is equal to the Father, when Jesus himself said, "The Father is greater than I" (*Jn* 14:28). Augustine helps us here.

Augustine concedes that many "statements in the Scriptures imply, or even openly assert, that the Father is greater than the Son." People have erred, though, in transferring "what is said of Christ Jesus as man to his mode of being before his incarnation, which was and is eternal."[7] Indeed, when Jesus states that "the Father is greater than I," Augustine teaches that "in this respect the Son is also inferior to himself. For if 'he emptied himself, receiving the form of a servant' (*Phil* 2:7), he must surely have become inferior to himself."[8]

The key to understanding who Jesus is – and to interpreting the Scriptures well – is to always bear in mind that in the movement of the Son into our world, *he becomes genuinely human,* while always remaining God.

---

7. Augustine, *The Trinity* 1.14; ACD 2.59-60.
8. Ibid.

Hence, it should not surprise us that some Scriptures speak of the Father as greater than the Son, for the Father did not become incarnate on our behalf. Only the Son is fully human, and fully God. The Father is surely greater than the incarnate Son as a human being, while the Son remains equal to the Father in his divine nature, for he is "true God from true God."

In the incarnation we behold the Son in two "forms": human and divine.

In both forms he was the same only-begotten Son of God the Father, in the form of God equal to the Father, in the form of a servant 'the mediator between God and humankind, the man Christ Jesus' (1 *Tim* 2:5). Then obviously in the form of a servant he is inferior to himself in the form of God . . . In the form of God he made humankind, in the form of a servant he was made man . . . Therefore since the form of God received the form of a servant, he is both God and man; but God because God took humanity; man, because of the taking of humanity. And by that taking neither is turned or changed into the other; Godhead is not changed into a creature, so as to cease to be Godhead, or creature into Godhead, so as to cease to be creature."[9]

Pause and reflect: I encourage you to ponder carefully and slowly the passage I just quoted from Augustine's *The Trinity*. If we understand Augustine's thought here, we can avoid much confusion about the incarnate Son – Jesus Christ – and about God. Let's break it down:

- Some Scriptures describe the Son as inferior to the Father.
- These Scriptures are referring to the Son's humanity.
- The Son in his divine nature is superior to the Son in his human nature. As Augustine puts it, "in the form of a servant he is inferior to himself in the form of God." Augustine feels this is an obvious point.
- The Son as God will never be changed into a human being. Instead, the Son's divine nature is joined to human nature in an ineffable or indescribable union.
- To sum up: the Son is true God, just as the Father is true God. The Son is "true God from true God."

---

9. Ibid.

4
BEGOTTEN, NOT MADE

Begotten, not Made

Admittedly, the language of the Son as "begotten" is at first glance strange. Why would the church fathers have chosen this language to describe the relationship between the Son and Father? Remember, the Father and Son are relationally distinct. The church fathers had to employ language that expressed this relational distinction and order well.

A creature is just that – a creature. A creature is distinct from God as created by God. At one point in time a creature did not exist. Then God created it. A creature is not eternal. It has a beginning and an end in time. A creature is distinct from and infinitely inferior to God, its creator.

The African fathers realized that certain terms are appropriate descriptors for relationships between God and God's creatures: creatures are "created," "made," and "timebound." Words such as these are fitting to describe human beings as God's image-bearers (cf. *Gen* 1:26). They are not suitable to describe the relationship between the Son as true God and the Father as true God. Can you see why?

Every word designating a relationship between God and a creature describes a relationship that is temporal. This works for creatures, for creatures exist in time. A rock exists in time. A star exists in time. A human being exists in time. Time is the water God has created for human beings to swim in.

When we endeavor to describe the relationship between the Father and Son, we realize straightaway that "time" language won't work. For God is eternal. The Father is eternal. The Son is eternal. The have always related to one another timelessly.

So, when the African fathers, and the church fathers as a whole, considered how to describe the eternal relationship between the Father and the Son, they knew they must be careful and precise. They finally chose the language of "begetting" and "begotten" to speak of this eternal relationship, but still realized they must express precisely what they understood these terms to mean – and not mean.

For instance, Athanasius writes that it "is right to call the Son the eternal offspring of the Father, for the substance of the Father was never imperfect so that what belonged to it might be added later. To beget in time is characteristic of humankind. For human nature is incomplete; God's offspring is eternal, for his nature is always perfect."[1]

* * *

Pause and reflect: Did you grasp Athanasius's point? It is correct to describe the Son as the "offspring" of the Father. Yet when we do so, we must immediately qualify what we mean by "offspring". The fact that the Father begets the Son does not indicate any imperfection in the Father that he is perfecting by later begetting the Son. No, the Father has always been "Father" to the "Son," who finds his eternal origin in the Father. The Father's begetting of the Son is an eternal begetting or generation. Admittedly, it will take some time to wrap our minds around an eternal begetting, for the only begetting we're familiar with is earthly fathers begetting children.

A human child does not come into existence until it's conceived in its mother's womb as the father's sperm fertilizes the mother's egg. This is not true of the begetting of the Son by the Father, for they have *always* been Father and Son. This is what God *is*. God *is* the Father and the Son and the Holy Spirit. The Father begets the Son timelessly, eternally.

Let's listen again to Athanasius. "Created things have come into being by God's pleasure and by his will, but the Son is not a creation of his will,

---

1. Athanasius, *Against the Arians* 1.14; ACD 2.62.

nor has he come into being subsequently, as the creation did. Rather, he is by nature the proper offspring of the Father's substance."[2]

* * *

Pause and reflect: The Father never decided to become a Father and to have a Son. Rather, God exists relationally as Father, Son, and Holy Spirit. All three persons share the same divine essence. *Take time to ponder this.* Try to list two implications of this truth.

* * *

The Father and the Son, along with the Holy Spirit, are relationally distinct within the "substance" or "essence" of God. When Christians speak of God as Trinity, they are referring to these relational distinctions: the Father is not the Son. The Son is not the Father. The Father is not the Holy Spirit. The Son is not the Holy Spirit. The Holy Spirit is not the Father. The Holy Spirit is not the Son. The three are relationally distinct, while remaining essentially one God.

Trinitarian language seems odd at first, for we don't normally use language this way. But it is correct when we use words to describe *relationships* within the Trinity, or in the case we are presently pondering, the begetting of the Son by the Father. The Son is "Begotten, Not Made."

Nothing exists before the Son, for the Son "is the proper Word of the Father," not willed into existence by the Father, but always existing as the Son, "since he is the Father's living counsel and power. . ." Consider John 1:1. "In the beginning *was* the Word. . ." Whenever the "beginning" began, the Son already "was", existing with the Father as the Father's eternal *logos* or Word, by whom the Father created all things, "fashioning what the Father had decided on . . . ."[3]

---

2. Athanasius, *Against the Arians* 3.63, 66; ACD 2.62.
3. Ibid.

ESSENTIAL ATTRIBUTES, ACCIDENTAL ATTRIBUTES, AND RELATIONAL PREDICATES WITHIN THE TRINITY

Let's pause for a moment to reflect on how we use words to describe a ball. A ball is a spherical object that can be kicked, thrown, or hit in a game, whether it is large or small, or red or yellow. Words like "large" or "small", or "red" or "yellow", don't describe the essential quality of what a ball *is*. To use technical language, they are "accidental attributes," attributes that are external to the essence of something, like a ball's size or color.

A ball may be large or small, red or yellow. It may be a baseball, a football, a golf ball. Its essence as a ball, however, never changes. Take time to ponder the difference between accidental attributes and essential attributes. Try to create another example than the one I have provided.

Now let's consider something quite important that the African father Augustine says about God. "Nothing is predicated of God *per accidens*, because nothing in him is subject to change."[4] For instance, God can't become larger or smaller. So, when we predicate things to be true of God, such as Father or Son, are we speaking of God's essence?

No, says Augustine. "Father" and "Son" are "relative predicates, as Father in relation to Son, Son in relation to Father." "Father" and "Son" are relational predicates. "[F]or the Father is always Father, the Son always Son." *This is an important point*, "for although being Son, Augustine writes, "is different from being Father, there is no difference of substance".[5]

Christians worship only one God, not three. Yet, as we've seen, there are relational distinctions that we recognize in God as Trinity. The Father is Father and not Son; the Son is Son and not Father. The Holy Spirit is neither Father nor Son. In Augustine's words, "those predicates are relative, yet not accidental, because they are not susceptible of change."[6]

Augustine believes that John 5:26 is helpful as we ponder the relationship between the Father and the Son and the nature of the Son as begotten. "For as the Father has life in himself, so he has granted the Son also to

---

4. Augustine, *The Trinity* 5.6; ACD 2.64
5. Ibid.
6. Ibid.

have life in himself." Does this text mean that before the Father granted life to the Son, the Son didn't "have life in himself"?

No, Augustine replies. "... it is not meant that the Father has given life to a Son who hitherto was lifeless, *but that he has begotten him timelessly,* in such a way that the life which the Father has given to the Son in begetting him is coeternal with the life of the Father who has given it."[7]

PSALM 110

Another key Bible text that received intense reflection and comment from the African fathers was Psalm 110:1, a text that Jesus discusses with the Pharisees in Matthew 22:41-45. "While the Pharisees were gathered together, Jesus asked them, 'What do you think about the Messiah? Whose son is he?' 'The son of David,' they replied. He replied to them, 'How is it then that David, speaking by the Spirit, calls him 'Lord'? For he says, 'The Lord said to my Lord: 'Sit at my right hand until I put your enemies under your feet.' If then David calls him 'Lord,' how can he be his son?'" Good question!

Do you see the problem the Pharisees faced? They – the teachers of Israel -- firmly believed that the Messiah would be David's son, his descendant. Yet here was David writing – by the Holy Spirit – that the Lord, David's Lord, would sit at God's right hand until his enemies had been defeated. If the Messiah was David's son, how could he be his Lord? *Only if the Messiah was much greater than the Pharisees and Israel as a whole expected him to be.*

Cyril of Alexandria rightly asks, "How, therefore, is the Son of David, David's Lord and seated also at the right hand of God the Father, and on the throne of Deity?"[8]

Cyril answers this question by pointing to the deity of the incarnate Word.

> Or is it not altogether according to the unerring word of the mystery, that the Word, being God, and sprung from the very substance of God the Father and being in his likeness and on an equality with him, became flesh,

---

7. Ibid., 15.47; ACD 2.64; my emphasis.
8. Cyril of Alexandria, *Homilies on the Gospel of Luke* 137; ACD 2.65.

that is man, perfectly so, and yet without departing from the incomparable excellence of the divine dignities, continuing rather in that estate in which he had ever been and still being God, though he had become flesh, and 'in form like us' (*Phil* 2:7-8)?[9]

That's one long sentence from Cyril! Let's break it down:

- The Word – the divine *logos* – is God.
- The Word shares the same substance or essence with God the Father.
- The Word is in the likeness of the Father, yet distinct from the Father.
- The Word is equal to the Father.
- The Word became "flesh," a human being, a perfect man.
- When the Word became a human being, he continued to be God. In Cyril's words, the Word continued "in that estate in which he had ever been, and still being God, though he had become flesh..."

David's son, then, was indeed, David's Lord, for God's Son entered the world as Jesus Christ, the incarnate Lord. Who is Jesus? The fully divine, fully human Lord. "He is David's Lord, therefore, according to that which belongs to his divine glory and nature and sovereignty, but David's son according to the flesh."[10]

Cyril of Alexandria's *Homilies on the Gospel of Luke*, from which I just quoted, are filled with many gems of wisdom. As I write today, Christmas is one week away, and Cyril's insights are encouraging me, all of them concerning the wonder of the incarnation.

Think of the birth of Jesus, the entrance of the eternal Son into the world. At that moment, human history's shattered story begins to be set right, as the healing antidote of Jesus' humanity is injected into the poisonous narrative inaugurated with Adam and Eve's fall into sin.

The birth of Jesus germinates the seeds of redemption, and the fruit of salvation appears in unexpected places. Gentiles, the well-known "wise

---

9. Ibid.
10. Ibid., 2; ACD 2.65.

men" or "magi" of the biblical narrative, come to worship the child laying in a feeding trough. They represent the entrance of Gentiles, too, into the kingdom of Israel's messiah. Cyril refers beautifully to the Magi in one of his homilies. "Their first fruits and leaders were the Magi, who came from the East to Jerusalem; whose teacher was the heaven, whose schoolmaster was a star."[11]

* * *

Pause and reflect: *Consider what Cyril is saying.* The heavens taught the Magi about the anointed one of Israel. The star that providentially guided them was their "schoolmaster." I think of the African sky I have seen on many occasions. When you travel away from big cities like Nairobi, Accra, or Kigali, the sky simply sparkles. Its beauty can still teach us much about the ways of God with his precious image-bearers. He spoke to the Wise Men. What has he been saying to you as we ponder the Nicene Creed with our African fathers? *If you were to make an "insight list" that you have gained from their teachings, what would be on it? What thoughts? Prayers? Ponderings? Insights?* Write them down.

* * *

DIVINE WISDOM ACCOMMODATES ITSELF TO HUMAN WISDOM IN THE INCARNATION

For a moment, let's continue to listen to Cyril's teaching concerning the one who was "begotten, not made." Because the incarnate Jesus was and is genuinely God, "he knew only the good and was exempt from that depravity that belongs to humanity." The Son, although fully human, was also divine, "good by nature, firmly and unchangeably." This pristine goodness is true only of God, "for there is none good, but one God, as the Savior has himself said" (*Lk* 18:19).[12]

Cyril notices that Luke "did not introduce the Word in his abstract and incorporeal nature." It is in Christ's human nature that "he increased in

---

11. Ibid., 2; ACD 2.65.
12. Ibid., 2; ACD 2.66.

stature and wisdom and grace" (*Lk* 2:52). God's wisdom can't increase, "for God is perceived by the understanding to be entirely perfect in all things and altogether incapable of being destitute of any attribute suitable to the Godhead."[13]

What cannot increase in God, however, can increase in the human nature the Son assumed in the incarnation. The eternal Word (*Jn* 1:1), indeed, "became flesh" in the womb of Mary. As Jesus grew and matured, Cyril believes his divine wisdom accommodated itself to the different stages of human growth that Jesus experienced. "God the Word gradually manifested his wisdom proportionally to the age the body had attained."[14]

When Jesus was an infant, God the Word manifested his wisdom proportionally through a baby's mind. Then a young boy's mind. Then a teenager's mind. Then a young man's mind. Then a mature Jewish rabbi's mind. How is this possible? Ah, such is possible through the incomprehensible wisdom of God. "And with good reason he connected the increase of wisdom with the growth of the bodily stature, because the divine nature revealed to the measure of the bodily growth."[15]

* * *

Pause and reflect: Follow Cyril's argument carefully. Take your time. The wisdom of the divine *logos* -- God the Word -- cannot increase. By definition, it is infinite and perfect. Yet, Cyril argues, what God amazingly accomplishes in the incarnation is the gradual increase in Jesus' human brain of the knowledge he possesses as God. We will continue to explore the implications of this expansion in Jesus' human knowledge. As a human being, he learns as a human being. As God he can't learn, for his divine knowledge is boundless. Still, in the humanity of Jesus and God's union with it, Jesus grows in wisdom and stature. Pray as you ponder this. Write down any insights that come, or questions.

* * *

---

13. Ibid.
14. Ibid.
15. Ibid., 5; ACD 2.67.

"EVERYTHING HAS BEEN DELIVERED TO ME BY MY FATHER"

Now, let's consider Cyril's interpretation of Jesus' words in Matthew 11:27. "Everything has been delivered to me by my Father." First, we must remember that Jesus, the incarnate Word, is one person, not two. Christ possesses two natures, one human and one divine. Yet the subject of those two natures, the person to whom they apply, is the one incarnate Lord. There is not one Lord to whom the attributes of the human nature apply, and another Lord to whom we attribute divine attributes. No, in the incarnate Word of God we encounter one person.

When Cyril interprets Jesus' words in Matthew 11:27, he encourages us to open "wide the eye of the mind." When we do so, Cyril believes we will understand Christ's words in a new way, in a manner appropriate to both his deity and his humanity.

Regarding Jesus' deity, Cyril writes, "For he was and still is Lord of heaven and earth, and sits with the Father on his throne and equally shares his government over all."[16] From Cyril's perspective, none of the divine attributes and prerogatives of God the Word ceased or changed when the Son was born at Bethlehem.

Cyril, however, continues to write, "inasmuch as he became man by humbling himself to our estate, he further speaks in a manner fitting to the dispensation in the flesh and does not refuse those expressions that suit the measure of his state, when he had emptied himself, that he might be believed on as having become like to us and having put on our poverty."[17]

In the "dispensation" of the flesh – the incarnation -- the Son truly becomes human and has a human name, Jesus of Nazareth. Thus, when Jesus speaks or the Scripture speaks of him, Cyril believes the words spoken sometimes signify his eternal existence as God the Word, and sometimes they refer to his humanity.

Thus, when Jesus speaks of all things having been delivered to him by his Father in Matthew 11:27, Cyril draws a number of interesting conclusions: "He, therefore, who was Lord of heaven and earth, and in a word, of all things, says that 'everything was delivered' to him by the by the Father.

---

16. Ibid., 66; ACD 2.67.
17. Ibid.

For he has been made ruler of all under heaven."[18] In the incarnate Son, the rule of God now fully extends to Jew and Gentile. It was never God's plan to bless only Israel. "God the Father willed to make all things new in him and by his means to reconcile the world to himself."[19]

In other words, Cyril believes, God's will for the entire world – and not only Israel – was to send the Son as the great reconciler and mediator. "For he became mediator between God and humanity and was made our peace, *in that he united us by himself to God the Father.*"[20] Cyril turns to Jesus' own teaching in John 14:6 to emphasize his point. "For he is the door and the way whereby this is done; for he has even plainly said, 'No man comes to the Father but by me.'"

Cyril explains that God's eternal purposes and actions *have broadened in their historical manifestation* through the incarnation of the Son. "He, then, who of old delivered Israel by the hand of Moses from the tyranny of the Egyptians and appointed the law to be their schoolmaster has now called the whole world. He himself has spread the net of the gospel message for it, according to the good will of God the Father. And this is the reason why he says, 'Everything has been delivered to me by my Father' (*Mt* 11:27)."[21]

When we consider the incarnation, we must keep two things in mind; Cyril helps us to do so. First, the Son who entered our world at Bethlehem is fully God, just as the Father is fully God. Second, the Son is begotten from the Father. The Father begets the Son.

> For he . . . by right of his nature possesses everything that God is, who begot him; by being of the selfsame substance, and of an equality admitting of no variation and of a similarity to him in everything. Being, therefore, by nature God, he is said to have received of the Father the 'name that is above every name,' when he had become man, that he might be believed in as God and the King of all, even in the flesh that was united to him.[22]

* * *

---

18. Ibid; my emphasis.
19. Ibid.
20. Ibid.
21. Ibid.
22. Ibid., 128; ACD 2.67.

Pause and reflect: *Ponder Cyril's last phrase*: "even in the flesh that was united to him." The God we worship is very earthy. He delights in using matter to create in many different ways. He created the universe. He created the planet earth. On this tiny planet he created all kinds of creatures. Anything created by God is a creature. Dirt is a creature. Water is a creature. Rock is a creature. Fish are creatures. Birds are creatures. Human beings are very exceptional creatures, for they bear the image of God in a special and unique way. And the incarnate Son of God is the most beautiful and unique creature of all (cf. *Col* 1:15 ff).

* * *

We recognize the distinctive creatures that we are from the first chapter of Genesis, where the writer presents human beings as the summit of God's creative endeavor, God's precious image-bearers (*Gen* 1:26).

When the original couple – Adam and Eve -- fell into sin, human nature became subject to corruption and death. It began to disintegrate. No longer was human nature whole, and healthy, what it was created by God to be. Athanasius emphasizes the corrupting effect of sin. This corruption results from the devastating decision of Adam and Eve to sin, one that they freely chose. No one forced them to do so.

HELP FROM ATHANASIUS: THE SON IS BEGOTTEN BY THE FATHER

Do you recall that the key issue at hand in the controversy with Arius concerns Christ's deity, which Arius denied. What was Arius's problem? To his mind, if the Son possessed the same nature as the Father – is "consubstantial" with him – then God's simplicity was threatened.

God's simplicity? To say that God is simple is to state that God is not made up of parts. God is not a composite being, composed out of something else, whatever that may be. Both Arius and Athanasius believed this to be true. In Arius's perspective, if God the Father had a Son who shared the same divine nature, this would mean "the Father is compound and divisible and alterable and a body. . ."[23] For bodies consist of different parts: blood flesh, bone, different organs, and so on.

Arius concludes on the basis of God's simplicity that whoever and whatever the Son is, he cannot be eternally God, uncreated and consubstantial with the Father, for this would mean that God has at least two parts, the Father and the Son. God would be compound, not simple.

To use an American expression, Arius wants to have his cake and eat it, too. On the one hand, he wants to say that the Son is "divine" in some sense of the word. On the other hand, he wants to preserve God's simplicity (God is not a composite being, made out of something prior to God) and indivisibility (God can't be divided into parts). If Arius affirms Christ's deity, it seems to him that both God's simplicity and indivisibility are lost.

Arius makes a bad theological move to solve the conundrum the deity of the Son poses. He asserts that the Son was "begotten timelessly by the Father and created before ages and established."[24] Arius affirms that the Son is utterly unique, *yet he believes the Son is still a creature*, "neither eternal nor coeternal nor co-unbegotten with the Father, nor does he have his being together with the Father."[25]

As much as Arius desires to elevate the status of the Son, he still argues that the Son is a creature who at one time did not exist. Arius creates an irresolvable problem for himself. For to worship a creature is to commit the sin of idolatry. Not only so, but can a creature save us from the ravages of sin?

The church will have to produce a better model of the incarnation than that offered by Arius. And so we turn our attention to the African Athanasius, archbishop of Alexandria during much of the Arian crisis. The question the church must prayerfully answer is how best to describe an incomprehensible mystery: God the Son as both divine and human.

In his response to Arius, Athanasius demonstrates his skill as a biblical interpreter, and profound theological insight.[26] Athanasius views Arius's

---

23. Arius, *The Confession of the Arians, Addressed to Alexander of Alexandria*, cited in Hardy, *Christology of the Later Fathers*, 333.
24. Arius, *Confession of the Arians*, cited in Hardy, *Christology of the Later Fathers*, 333.
25. Ibid.
26. For a brief biographical note on Athanasius, see Christopher A. Hall, *Reading Scripture with the Church Fathers* (Downers Grove: IVP Academic, 1998), 56-57.

position as fundamentally flawed. In his great work *Orationes contra Arianos (Orations Against Arius)*, Athanasius discusses the implications of Arius's assertion that the Son of God is an elevated, unique creature who was created timelessly by God.

Athanasius asks us to consider the names the Son is given in Holy Scripture. He is called "Son," "God," and "Wisdom." How could the Son receive names such as these if he was a only a creature, elevated though he might be? Arius had suggested that these names could be applied to the Son because he *participates* in the Holy Spirit. In this *participation*, the Holy Spirit communicates to the Son attributes *the Son does not possess by nature*.

Does Arius's proposal succeed in accomplishing what Arius intends? Athanasius is unconvinced. Athanasius points to John's gospel. Doesn't Arius's understanding of participation and communion reverse what we find in John, for there we find Jesus teaching that the Spirit "will glorify me, because he will take what is mine and declare it to you" (*Jn* 16:14). Athanasius is willing to agree that the Son does receive by participation, but in an eternal, *essential* participation, one that has always characterized the relationship *between Father and Son*. "This is the only possibility."[27]

Arius had pictured the Father and Son as bottles or decanters that fill each other, similar to how God's saints experienced participation in God when filled with the Holy Spirit. In this way, Arius believes he has preserved the uniqueness of God, while elevating the status of the Son above all other creatures. When he reads Jesus' teaching to Philip in John 14:10, "I am in the Father and the Father is in me", Arius interprets Jesus' words as indicating participation in the Spirit. Arius describes this participation as similar to what other human beings occasionally experience. The Son's participation, though, is greater and deeper than that of other creatures.

Athanasius will have none of this. Athanasius writes:

> I in the Father and the Father in me does not mean (as the Arians suppose) that they are decanted into each other, being each filled from the other, as in the case of empty vessels, so that the Son fills the Father's emptiness,

---

27. Athanasius, *Four Discourses Against the Arians*, 1.15, cited in Henry Bettenson, ed. and trans., *The Early Christian Fathers: A Selection from the Writings of the Fathers from St. Clement of Rome to St. Athanasius* (London: Oxford University Press, 1956), 381.

and the Father the Son's, each of them separately not being full and perfect ... for the Father is full and perfect, and the Son is 'the fullness of the Godhead' (*Col* 2:9). Again, God is not in the Son in the same way as he comes into the saints and thus strengthens them.[28]

* * *

Pause and reflect: Did you understand Athanasius' point? God pours the Spirit into a human such as Isaiah. For Isaiah to speak the word of the Lord, he must be filled with the Holy Spirit. There is no similar emptiness in either the Father or the Son. Each is completely, infinitely full, and share in each other's fullness.

Athanasius urges his readers to shatter the image of the Son or the Father as empty decanters or bottles; the Son has no need to be filled with the Father for he is already boundlessly and timelessly filled with the Father's fullness. There has never been a moment when the Son was not full. There is nothing in the Son that needs filling.

Take a moment to reflect on the difference between the positions proposed by Athanasius and Arius. Who do you feel is most convincing? Why? Write out what your response would be to Arius, and to Athanasius. The church in the Nicene Creed affirms its belief that Athanasius got things right.

* * *

AN ETERNAL PARTICIPATION

Arius stumbles because his vision of God's glory is blurry at best. He sees the glory of God the Father, but does not understand how this glory could possibly be shared with the Son if the oneness of God and God's simplicity is to be maintained.

The only alternative Arius can conceive is to picture the Son as a creature. This simply doesn't work. Athanasius discerns the salvation of the world at stake. How so? Only God can save. Hence, the Son must be God.

If Arius's understanding of participation is faulty, what does Athana-

---

28. Ibid., 1.14, 393-394.

sius offer instead? He understands correctly that the "partaking" or "sharing" must be eternal in nature and must be a sharing in "the substance of the Father," as difficult this may be for us to conceive. This a participation that is interior between the Father and the Son, rather than exterior. If it was an exterior participation, it would by definition be outside of the filial relationship of the Son to the Father.

Do you perceive the unique relationship the Son has with the Father? The Father begets the Son in an eternal, incomprehensible generation. In turn, the Son is eternally begotten by the Father. In describing this relationship, we neither want to say too much, or say too little.

* * *

Pause and reflect: Note this very carefully. The eternal reality of God as Father demands that he have a Son eternally in relationship with him. The relationship between the Father and Son never begins and will never end. Try to write a paragraph describing the relationship between the Father and Son in your own words.

* * *

The Nicene Creed describes the relational distinction between the Father and the Son with the language of "unbegotten" – the Father – and "begotten" – the Son. These descriptors reflect the language of the Bible and are appropriate to describe the personal relationship that exists between the Father and Son. Think of the apostle John's words in John 3:16. I'll bet they're beginning to take on new significance in your mind and heart. "For God so loved the world that he gave his only begotten Son, that whoever believes in him should not perish but have everlasting life."

"Only begotten" does not refer to a sexual begetting, which some confused, ancient Christians thought. No, no. It refers to the unique status of the Son of God. Modern translations capture its meaning well. For instance, the New International Version translates, "his one and only Son." The New Revised Version renders "his only Son." Both translations stress that the eternal Son of God is unique. No other relationship matches that between the Father as "unbegotten" and the Son as "begotten".

*   *   *

Pause and reflect: Memorize the following italicized sentence: *An eternal Father must have an eternal Son.* Was, Athanasius asks, God ever without his Word? How could he be? Athanasius employs the illustration we have earlier encountered in this book. "Was he, who is light, without radiance . . . God is, eternally; then since the Father always is, his brightness exists eternally."[29] Athanasius continues: "If a man looked at the sun and asked about its radiance, 'Did that which 'is' make something which did not exist before, or something which already existed [a frequent Arian question regarding the Father and the Son] he would not be regarded as reasoning sensibly; he would in fact be crazy in supposing that what comes from the light is external to it."[30]

*   *   *

Just as the sun is inseparable from its rays – to be the sun is to shed light – likewise, for the Father to be Father is to have a Son. How could things be otherwise? The begetting of the Son is internal to the relationship between the Father and the Son, not external. The analogy of the sun and its rays is helpful. Athanasius explains:

We see that the radiance of the sun is integral to it, and that the substance of the sun is not divided or diminished; but its substance is entire, and its radiance perfect and entire, and the radiance does not diminish the substance of the light, *but is as it were a genuine offspring from it. Thus we see that the Son is begotten not from without,* but 'from the Father,' and that the Father remains entire, while the 'stamp of his substance' (*Heb* 1:3) exists always and preserves the likeness and image without alteration.[31]

Athanasius's argument and illustration run against the grain of the Arian insistence that the generation of the Son – to be begotten is to be generated – is external to the Father, that is, a generation that takes place at some "time," even if that time is before the creation of the heavens and

---

29. Ibid., 1.25, 382.
30. Ibid.
31. Ibid., 2.33, 390; my emphasis.

the earth. As long as Arius insists that there was a time when the Son did not exist, such must be the case. Hence, Athanasius's continuing use of the illustration of the sun and its rays makes sense. The two are inseparable, as are the Father and the Son.

Athanasius links the confusion of the Arian position to the types of questions they pose. Arian questions are formed on the basis of what is possible within the boundaries of creation. For instance, if human begetting occurs within time, Arians reason, so must heavenly begetting. If such is the case, how can the Son exist eternally with the Father? No human son exists before his father begets him. So how can God's Son eternally exist? Things don't work this way in creation.

The Arian line of reasoning demonstrates Athanasius's point. The Arians are asking the wrong kinds of questions because the starting point for their questioning is *what is possible within the created order*. Their questions and ponderings should begin, though, with *what's possible for God and what God has said regarding his Son*. Start with what is possible for God, not what is possible within the laws of creation. Questions posed on the basis of this principle will be wise, not foolish.

If the Arians fail to heed these guidelines, they will continue to misunderstand the personal relations within the Trinity. They will infer wrongly that since human procreation takes place in time and space, so must the begetting of the Son. Not so, Athanasius insists. The begetting of the Son is interior to the Father and the Son, not exterior where the laws of the created order would be appropriately applicable.

The Arians have misunderstood the subject of the begetting of the Son. The unbegotten Father begets the Son. "The character of the parent determines the character of the offspring. Man is begotten in time and begets in time; he comes into being from non-existence."[32] Not so with the divine begetting, which is unique and unlike human begetting.

The Arians have committed a serious category error. *They have applied human categories to God in an inappropriate and illogical fashion.* "God," Athanasius insists, "is not like man."[33] Rather, "he is 'he who exists' (*Ex* 3:14) and exists forever." Furthermore, "his Word is 'that which exists,' and exists eternally with the Father, *as radiance from a light* . . . But God's word

---

32. Ibid; my emphasis.
33. Ibid.

is not merely 'emitted,' as one might say, nor is it just an articulate noise; nor is 'the Son of God' just a synonym for the command of God,' but he is the perfect offspring of the perfect."[34]

God's divine Word – now fully present in union with the human nature of Jesus, the incarnate *Logos* -- is unique and unlike human words. A human word is spoken into the air and disappears with the speaking. Human words at one time don't exist, and cease to exist once they are spoken. How different with God's eternal Word! For this Word has always been with the Father, is now present, and will always be present. There is no other word like this in all the created order.

The Arians have made a fundamental mistake by imagining God's Word – the divine *Logos* – to have the characteristics of a human word. If this was true, what is possible or impossible for human words would also be true of God's Word.

The same is true of the Arian view of Jesus, whom they deny is God. "Now if they are discussing a *man*," Athanasius argues, "then they may argue about his word and his son on the human level. But if they are talking of God, man's creator, they must not think of him on the human level."[35]

"God," Athanasius teaches, "is not like man." Rather, "he is 'he who exists' (*Ex* 3:14) and exists forever." Likewise, "his Word is 'that which exists,' and exists eternally with the Father, *as radiance from a light*."[36]

God does not speak his Word so that the Word as a subordinate might carry it out. No, "this is what happens in human affairs. But the Word of God is creator and maker, and he *is* the Father's will."[37]

* * *

Pause and reflect: Always beware of *theological and spiritual presumption*, which seems to characterize the Arian approach in its inquiries, questions, and statements about God. How does this presumption manifest itself? They tend to ask the wrong questions or ask questions that should be posed with greater reverence. What are the questions you ask about God?

---

34. Ibid, my emphasis.
35. Ibid; 2.35, 391.
36. Ibid, my emphasis.
37. Ibid; 2.31, 390.

Do they reflect an unbridled curiosity? Do you pose them from your desk as you study, or from your knees as you pray? Surround your study – and the questions you ask – with prayer and worship. Describe your approach to your work as you study God.

* * *

Consider common Arian questions: Why is the Word of God not like human words? How is the Word of God from God? How is the Word God's radiance? How does God beget? What is the manner of God's begetting? These questions themselves may be valid. But do they demonstrate an unrestrained curiosity, one that recognizes no limits? Athanasius thinks so.

"It is enough merely to write down the kind of things they say," Athanasius scolds, "to show their reckless impiety. They ask such nonsensical questions as, 'Has he free will, or not?' 'Is he good from choice, of free will, and can he change, if he so will, being by nature capable of change?' . . . It is blasphemy to utter such things."[38]

Athanasius is convinced that the Arians employ language in a purposely deceitful manner:

> Let us look at the replies which the Arians gave to Alexander (who is now in peace) at the beginning, when their heresy was being formed. They wrote, 'He is a creature, but not as one of the creatures; a work, but not as one of the works; an offspring, but not as one of the offsprings.' . . . What is the use of this disingenuous talk, saying that he is 'a creature and not a creature'?[39]

Athanasius discerns theological pride and irreverence lurking behind the manner and content of the Arian questions. To be fair, when we critique Arian questions, we must ask ourselves what kinds of questions we pose to ourselves or to others about God. How did our own questions arise? What affect do they have on how we pray? Or on how we worship?

We will always have questions about God. This is proper and good.

---
38. Ibid., 1.35, 383.
39. Ibid., 2.19, 387.

Sometimes, though, the line between an honest, searching question and a superficial, shallow, irreverent question can be very thin. So much depends on our motivation in asking. Are we genuinely seeking a deeper knowledge and love for God, or have we come to love theological debate and controversy? If we are less apt to worship because of our theological speculations and questions, it's time to hit the pause button.

*　*　*

Pause and reflect: Ask the Lord to help you discern the state of your own heart. Are you serious about your questions, or simply trying to win a theological debate? When posing them, have you acknowledged that God is an incomprehensible mystery? As Athanasius explains, the proud questions of the Arians "demand to have explained in words something ineffable and proper to God's nature, known only to him and to the Son."[40]

*　*　*

THE SMELL OF COFFEE

Words are delicate and fragile. They can only bear so much weight. When we load too much on them, they crack under the burden. The philosopher Ludwig Wittgenstein demonstrated how limited language is to express even the most common and simple phenomena. For example, ponder the following question and then try to answer it as clearly as you can without using the word "coffee." What does coffee smell like?

When I've posed this question to beginning theology students, I've received very surprising answers. Here are a few: "dirt", "warmth," "a spring morning," "something sweet," "something bitter," "wet mud." Now add your answer to the same question. What does coffee smell like?

Some of the most common human experiences, it seems, are incapable of precise description. Only linguistic turns of phrase like metaphor and simile suffice. How much more so, Athanasius argues, when we're dealing with God. God's wonder and beauty lie beyond precise description. When

---

40. Ibid., 2.36; 392.

we forget this in our theological study and formulations, we veer off course, and venture into dangerous terrain.

The Arians had forgotten with whom they are dealing. They had veered off course in their speculations and language. They demonstrate a theological and spiritual malaise traceable to a serious spiritual malady Athanasius diagnoses as "a lack of reverence and ignorance of God."[41] When we describe God through human concepts and language, we must humbly acknowledge language's limitations. Our practices and words in worship provide helpful bumper guards for our theological speculations.

Athanasius understood that the church's words and actions in worship must govern the beliefs it expressed outside of worship. For instance, from its earliest years the church had worshiped Jesus as God. Hence, Arius's proposals about the deity of Christ must be wrong and were finally rejected by the church as it gathered as a community in council. The result was the Nicene Creed.

Let's now review the ground we have traversed so far with Athanasius and other African fathers:

- The Son shares in the substance of the Father "as radiance from light, and stream from source . . . For the Father is in the Son as the sun is in its radiance, the thought in the word, the source in the stream."[42]
- The Son is both *in* the Father substantially and derives his being *from* the Father. The Father is the origin of the Son. The Father generates the Son. In the words of the Nicene Creed, the Son "is begotten, not made." This is surely a biblical statement. Both John 10:10, "the Father and I are one," and John 14:10, "I am in the Father and the Father is in me," indicate in Athanasius's words, "the identity of the godhead and the unity of the substance."
- We have considered errors that predictably occur if the relationship between the Son and Father is not carefully articulated. A frequent mistake I've encountered from my students is their tendency to picture each person of the Trinity

---

41. Ibid.
42. Ibid., 3.3, 394.

as a part of God. We've learned in this book, though, that God does not have parts. The Father is not part of God. The Son is not part of God. The Holy Spirit is not part of God. Rather, as Athanasius understood, they are "one thing."[43] God does not have parts, as though God were a composite being built out of ontic building blocks. This is what the church fathers mean when they describe God as indivisible. If indivisible, God is simple, not composite.

- Another error Athanasius combatted is to think that the essential unity of the Father and Son means there is no relational distinction between them. "Father" and "Son" merely become "two names" with no difference between them, "one thing with two names . . . the Son at one time Father, at another time his own Son." The names "Father" and "Son" become masks that God assumes in different points in human history as his plan for humanity proceeds in time. When the role God plays as "Father" ceases with the incarnation, God puts on a different mask, that of the Son. We encounter these ideas, Athanasius writes, in the thoughts of Sabellius, an ancient Christian heretic. No, Athanasius teaches, "they are two, in that the Father is father and not also son; the Son is son and not also father, but the nature is one."[44] The Nicene Creed affirms the essential or substantial unity of the Father and Son *and* their genuine relational distinction. The Father generates the Son, and not vice-versa.

The language of "begotten not made" emphasizes that the relational distinction between Father and Son demonstrates a clear order. The Son is begotten, the Father begets. To speak technically, the deity of the Son finds its source or fount in the deity of the Father. As the "offspring" of the Father, the Son is indeed relationally distinct, yet with the unity of God still maintained. The church worships one God, not three. In the Holy Trinity we have unity of essence, but relational distinctions. Let's listen again to Athanasius:

---

43. Ibid., 3.4, 395.
44. Ibid.

"For the radiance also is light, not a second light besides the sun, nor a different light, nor a light by participation in the sun, but a whole proper offspring of it. No one would say that there are two lights, but that the sun and its radiance are two, while the light from the sun, which illuminates things everywhere, is one. In the same way the godhead of the Son is the Father's."[45]

Remember, too, Athanasius's insistence that whatever is predicated of the Father can rightly be said of the Son, "except the title of 'Father.'" That is, if the Father is sovereign, so is the Son. If the Father is Lord, so is the Son. If the Father is light, so is the Son. "Thus, since they are one, and the godhead itself is one, the same things are predicated of the Son as of the Father, except for the title of 'Father.'"[46]

GENDERED LANGUAGE AND GOD

Some readers may find Nicene theology intimidating and overly technical. Others, though, may resist thinking of God as "Father" because of the abuse they have received – verbal or otherwise -- from their earthly fathers. The good news is that God, the source of all light, life, and love, as "Father" is the exact opposite of an evil father. What advice might Athanasius offer to those who have suffered abuse?

I think Athanasius would emphasize that words such as *Father* and *Son* are words that God in the Scripture chose as best to describe a relationship that in reality is indescribable or ineffable. That is, out of the various linguistic alternatives available to the church to describe relations within the Godhead, God selected through apostolic testimony certain words that describe intratrinitarian relationships more effectively than others.

Some of Athanasius's Greek opponents, for example, felt that words such as "Unoriginate" rather than "Father" eliminated the theological conundrums and confusion gendered language presented. Athanasius objected to such a move.

First, Athanasius argued that the words we find in the Bible are better than non-biblical ones. if we substitute "Unoriginate" for "Father", we use

---

45. Ibid.
46. Ibid.

"unscriptural" language. The use of "Father", Athanasius argues, is "simple and scriptural and more accurate."[47]

Athanasius is concerned that if we substitute words such as "Unoriginate" or "Maker" in place of "Father," we will create a model of God that doesn't represent clearly or safely what God has revealed about himself in Holy Scripture. "Unoriginate," a word that would communicate well to many Greeks, nevertheless fails to picture or describe adequately the wonder and beauty of the *personal communion* between Father, Son, and Holy Spirit.

Athanasius is aware that certain aspects of the word "Father" when used to describe human relationships *don't apply when referring to God*. In fact, the Arians consistently misunderstand Athanasius's point. We've seen that they misconstrue how human language and conceptual models apply to divine realities. God as "Father," for instance, does not beget the Son as human fathers produce children through sexual relations with their wives. No, God has *always* had a Son. For God has always been, is, and always will be "Father."

The Son is "the eternal offspring" of the Father. We rightfully conclude that whatever the generation of the Son means, it cannot mean that the Father generated the Son as a human father procreates children. An eternal Father is never without his Son, just as the sun cannot exist without its rays.

How might the thought of Athanasius help someone who has experienced abuse from their father, as happens often in Africa and around the world? He would emphasize that while human fathers can sin greatly, such is impossible for God. And then Athanasius would offer a series of contrasts that might prove helpful to those who have been abused.

A human father, in distinction from God the Father, is created, finite, fallen, human, male, and begets offspring through sexual relations. All human fathers are infected with sin and apt to manifest that sinfulness in horrible ways. A catalogue of abuse characterizes fallen human fatherhood in its worst moments.

When Athanasius and the Nicene Creed apply the word "Father" to God, some aspects of human fatherhood apply, and some don't. The idea of a good

---

47. Athanasius, *Four Discourses Against the Arians*, 1.34, trans. J.H. Newman, rev. A. Robertson, NPNF 4 (Peabody: Hendrickson, 1994), 326.

father as a protector or provider comes to mind as appropriate for us to apply. Other aspects of human fatherhood will have to be discarded. God is not an exploitive, abusive male. God is not finite, human, male, or infected with sin. God does not beget sons or daughters through sexual procreation. The Son is "begotten, not made."

"Father" and "Son" indicate that God is much more relationally complex than we would ever have imagined. They teach us that God is personal, more personal than we are as his precious image bearers. God is immensely, intensely personal.

* * *

Pause and reflect: Are you perceiving that it is easier to explain what we don't mean when we speak of God as Father than to explain well what we do mean? This is often the case when we use human language to express divine realities. The language we employ in describing God as Trinity is always limited in what it can express, for the Trinity is an *incomprehensible* wonder and beauty.

Picture words such as "Father" and "Son" as authoritative, verbal gifts given to us by God. God has chosen how he wishes to be described. "Father" and "Son" point beyond themselves to the mysterious, ineffable, personal communion present at the core of all reality.

Have you pictured God as an abusive father because of the language used in the Bible and Nicene Creed? Offer this warped picture of God to the true, infinitely loving Father. Ask for healing and protection from the hurts of the past or present. God the Father will respond. He is what we all hope all good earthly fathers to be, and much, much more.

We are personal and rational creatures, like angels and unlike trees, fish, or dogs. We reflect a bit of the immensely personal light that radiates from the Father and Son, for God is love and God is light.

Trinitarian language points to yet another marvel. Not only is God as Trinity a communion of love, but God has always existed in just such a way. God has always been and will always be Father. He did not become Father at a certain point in time. There has never been a single moment when God was not Father. It follows that God the Father must eternally have a Son, the Son who finds his origin in the Father, a Son generated by the Father eternally, ineffably, and incomprehensibly.

* * *

WE ARE GOD'S PRECIOUS IMAGE-BEARERS

Cyril of Alexandria explores the relational implications of God the Son as the only begotten Son of the Father, and links them to the creation of human beings in the image of God. First, Cyril reminds us that every human being is created in the image of God (*Gen* 1:26). And who is the preeminent image of God? The only begotten Son. Cyril writes:

> Now the image of God the Father is the Son (cf. *Col* 1:15) to whom we too have been conformed spiritually (cf. *Rom* 8:29), and human nature was enriched by this in an exceptional way, *for it was illuminated by the beauty radiating from the Creator*. What then can be said by those who oppose our ideas and make a pretense of piety by confessing with us that God is one and alone, yet maintain that the Son was not begotten from him? To whom did God say: 'Let us make God in our own image'?[48]

To confess that God is "one and alone," then, is not to exclude the confession that the Son is begotten from the Father.

Cyril discerns an important truth regarding the human nature that the eternally begotten Son has assumed in the incarnation. Human nature, the nature that you and I possess, "has been illuminated by the beauty radiating from the Creator." How so? The only begotten Son has joined his divine nature to our human nature and enriches that nature – Cyril uses the metaphor of illumination and radiation – through the union itself. Why does the Son do this? Because the Son -- along with the Father and the Holy Spirit -- loves human beings. We are God's precious image-bearers.

Picture our union with the incarnate Son – Jesus – as symbiotic. What Jesus said and did during his earthly life flowed out of his relationship with the Father, a relationship we experience with him through our baptism.

---

48. Cyril of Alexandria, *Against Julian*, in *Cyril of Alexandria*, Norman Russell (London and New York: Routledge, 2000), 196; I have very slightly modified the translation. The italics are mine.

Erasmo Leiva-Markakis conveys this relational intimacy well.

> By revealing the Father through every incident, word, and gesture of his life, Jesus is most fundamentally revealing the fact that God, in himself, is Love Relation and that everything else in Christianity flows from this truth. We cannot know how to interpret and live Jesus' teachings without, first, understanding something about *who Jesus is* and then, crucially, by *coming into a living symbiosis with him*. We can do what Jesus teaches only as a result of entering into an intimate union with his Divine Person, a union so intimate that it transforms its subject into a living member of Christ's very Body.[49]

All analogies and metaphors fall short at this point, for we have nothing in the created order that can adequately describe the personal communion we worship as God the Holy Trinity, and the depth of the relationship to which we are invited by God. How can we speak of such a mystery at all, especially if God has revealed it as indescribable?

We do so because God has spoken and acted. And what has God revealed to us? He has revealed himself as immensely personal mystery. We most clearly receive and speak God's language about God and us – we his precious image-bearers -- in worship, in the liturgy of the church, on our knees rather than in our studies.

* * *

Pause and reflect: In Athanasius's time, he was forced to say more about God than he would have liked, because other teachers were speaking of the mystery of God in such a way that the gospel was desperately threatened. Can you hear Athanasius's voice? I hear him growling. A paraphrase of his thoughts might sound like this: "How could I remain silent when Arius began to teach that the Son is an exalted creature? Can a creature save us from sin? Reverent silence and adoration is much more the proper response to the wonder and mystery of God. But there comes a time to speak, if only to build a conceptual and linguistic boundary around the

---

49. Erasmo Leiva-Merikakis, *Fire of Mercy, Heart of the Word: Meditations on the Gospel according to Saint Matthew*, Volume 4 (San Francisco: Ignatius Press, 2021), 83.

mystery itself. This is what I've attempted to do. God has chosen to manifest his love to us by sending his Son into our world. But God could only do so if he is genuinely Father, Son, and Holy Spirit."[50] What comes into your mind and heart as you reflect on Athanasius's thoughts? Write down two or three ideas or insights that come to mind.

* * *

---

50. In this section on "begotten, not made," I have drawn on the outline and thoughts I present in *Learning Theology with the Church Fathers,* published by IVP Academic, chapter two. I have significantly developed them, though.

5
ONE WITH THE FATHER

... of One Being with the Father

The Son shares "one being with the Father". The Son is *homoousios* with the Father, sharing the same or identical divine essence. How can this be? In this one phrase, the Nicene Creed expresses the mystery and beauty in three Greek words (*homoousion tō patri*), two in Latin (*consubstantialem Patri*), and six in English (*of one being with the Father*). These words declare the unity of God and also speak of the relational complexity we have discussed in this book.

Why these particular words, this specific phrase? This phrase in the Nicene Creed is a response to those who supported Arius's claim that the Son "was from nothing," that he "did not exist before he was begotten." No, Athanasius writes. To be begotten from the Father is to participate "in the substance of the Father," a substantial or essential unity that is eternal.[1] The union between the Father and the Son is *eternal, substantial, and internal*. The Father and Son shared this union before there ever was a "beginning." The union indicates that God is infinite, immense, intense, intimate personal communion.

---

1. Athanasius, *Against the Arians*, 1.15-16; ACD 2.69.

HELP FROM BASIL THE GREAT

Basil the Great helpfully explains the meaning of *homoousios* (Gk.) or "same essence". He writes, "the expression is sound and reverent, since it establishes the distinctive marks of the subsistences" – the persons – "while asserting they do not differ in nature."[2]

Basil explains that

> when we are told that the Son is 'of the substance of the Father', 'begotten, not made,' we must beware of lapsing into ideas of some kind of physical process. There is no division of substance, as if it were taken from the Father and given to the Son; nor did the substance generate by a process of change or by production, like a plant bearing fruit.[3]

* * *

Pause and reflect: Listen carefully to Basil. There is "no division of substance" between the Father and the Son. If there were, we could conceive the Father as part of God, sharing in part of the substance of God, and likewise with the Son. This would be a grave error. God does not have parts. God is simple. We must not chop God up into pieces, with the Father as "part" of God and the Son as another "part." In fact, to think this way about God is to be guilty of an early Christian heresy known as "partialism." God is not a composite being. God is simple and noncomposite, and eternally so.

The Son is not part of God. The Son is entirely God, sharing the same substance with the Father. Take a moment to pray through the wonder and beauty these truths represent. Do you find them troubling and unnecessarily abstract? Or surprisingly beautiful, as some mathematicians describe the exploration of a complex problem, even if they cannot solve its mystery? Write down your concerns, questions, and perceptions. Keep these before you as you continue to read.

* * *

---

2. Basil the Great, *Letter* 52.3; ACD 2.71; I have slightly modified the translation.
3. Ibid.

Basil writes that the Son is not produced "like a plant bearing fruit." A plant produces fruit sequentially in time. *First* a seed is planted, *then* germinates, and *finally* grows into a plant. *In turn*, fruit is produced or birthed by the plant. Every word I have italicized is a time word. Basil rightly insists that the begetting of the Son is nothing like a plant bearing fruit. In this case, the illustration of a plant bearing fruit doesn't help us to understand the Trinitarian mystery. As Basil teaches, "the mode of divine generation is ineffable and inconceivable by human thought."[4]

INSIGHTS FROM HEBREWS 1

Athanasius selects three verses from Hebrews 1 to emphasize a key point about the Son. "But of the Son he says, 'Your throne, O God, is forever and ever, and the righteous scepter is the scepter of your kingdom'" (1:8). "And, 'in the beginning, Lord, you founded the earth, and the heavens are the work of your hands; they will perish, but you remain; they will all wear out like clothing'" (1:10-11). These verses, in Athanasius's words, plainly show that "the Maker is different from his works."[5]

The Arians, of course, had insisted that the Son is a work of God, the highest and holiest creature ever made by the Father. No, Athanasius hears the writer of Hebrews proclaiming. ".... the Maker is different from his works. He is God, while they come into being and are made out of nothing."[6]

When creatures die, they show "the nature of created things by expressing their end." Not all creatures die, but "they are capable of destruction." They were created from nothing "and in themselves testify that once they did not exist, even though because of the grace of their maker they do not in fact perish."[7]

How different with the Son! Hebrews states "'you remain,' to show his eternity..."[8] To say, as the Arians do, that the Son "did not exist before his generation, is a statement alien to him. It is proper to him to exist always

---

4. Ibid.
5. Athanasius, *Against the Arians* 1.58; ACD 2.73.
6. Ibid.
7. Ibid.
8. Ibid.

and to 'remain,' together with the Father . . . He is *proper to the Father's substance and one in nature with it.*"[9]

In response to Athanasius's arguments, his Arian opponents frequently turned to Jesus' words that "the Father is greater than I" (*Jn* 14:28). If so, the Arians concluded the Son must be a creature. Athanasius response? The Arians are not reading the Scripture well. Jesus did not say the Father is greater to cast doubt on the divine nature he shares with the Father. No, this difference in greatness points to the Father as the origin of the Son. ". . . greater, that is, not in size or in virtue of duration but because of his begetting from the Father. In fact, by saying 'greater' he again shows that he is proper to the substance of the Father."[10] So, Athanasius says, it is fine for Jesus to say the Father is greater, both because the Son is generated by the Father and finds his source in him; in other places Athanasius turns to the wonder of the incarnation. For the Son in his deity is greater than the Son in his humanity, as is the Father.

* * *

Pause and reflect: Are the African fathers' comments on this section of the Nicene Creed making sense to you? The Son is "begotten, not made," a statement concerning the internal relationship between the Father and the Son within the mystery of the Holy Trinity.

There is a clear order in Trinitarian relationships. The Father begets the Son, and the Son is begotten. Yet the begetting of the Son is eternal, outside of time, and unlike normal begetting. For the Son exists in an eternal relation of love to the Father as the Father's beloved, only begotten Son. The Son shares the same nature as the Father. Or to use the exact words of the Nicene Creed, the Son "is of one being with the Father." Take a moment to ponder and pray. Write down any insights that come.

* * *

---

9. Ibid.
10. Ibid.

"THROUGH HIM ALL THINGS WERE MADE"

We now come to our next phrase: "Through Him all things were made." This clause of the Nicene Creed finds its biblical basis in two key texts:

John 1:3 – "Through him all things were made; without him nothing was made that has been made." (NIV)

Colossians 1:16 – "For in him all things were created: things in heaven and on earth, visible and invisible, whether thrones or powers or rulers or authorities; all things have been created through him and for him." (NIV)

ORIGEN, ATHANASIUS, AUGUSTINE, AND CYRIL OF ALEXANDRIA

Now let's examine the thoughts of four African church fathers -- Origen, Athanasius, Augustine, and Cyril of Alexandria. -- as they pondered these two texts.

Origen comments that "all things", a phrase that occurs in both John 1:3 and Colossians 1:16, includes "supernatural powers" such as angels. As powerful as these powers are, "Paul insists that they are subordinate to Christ's power and authority."[11]

Everything that exists – including angelic powers -- derives its being from the eternal *logos*, the Word (1:1-3). God's *logos*, now incarnate in Jesus Christ, has created all things. Athanasius comments that everything has been created "with meaning and purpose." God's *logos* "is the Son of God by nature proper to his essence and is from him," and hence the proper agent through whom all creation occurs.[12]

As a result of the Word's creative work, every aspect of creation has "meaning and purpose." I experienced this in an African context. Some Kenyan friends and I decided to drive south from Nairobi to Amboseli National Park. As we entered the park, animals started to appear. There, on the road directly in front of us, stood a giraffe. We encountered other animals: a lion hidden in the bush, an elephant to the right of our van, and a nearby rhino with his head down and eyes focused on us. He seemed to

---

11. Origen, *On First Principles* 4.4.3; ACCS NT IX, *Colossians, 1-2 Thessalonians, 1-2 Timothy, Titus, Philemon,* edited by Peter Gorday (Downers Grove: InterVarsity Press, 2000), 15.
12. Athanasius, *Discourses Against the Arians* 2.18.31; ACCS NT 9.15.

be warning us to keep our distance. Athanasius is right. God created all these creatures with "meaning and purpose."

* * *

Pause and reflect: Consider the millions of creatures God has created, all of them described as 'good' in the Genesis creation accounts (*Gen* 1:22, 25) A recent study estimates that the world contains 8.7 million species. Cataloging them all would take more than a thousand years. All of these creatures – reptiles, bugs, birds, mammals, amphibians, and single-cell creatures, are God's creation, God's delight. Take time to ponder and thank God for the meaning and purpose evident in creation. List aspects of creation that you especially delight in.

* * *

Augustine connects the prologue to John's gospel with John 8:58: "Before Abraham was born, I am!" Not only did Jesus exist before Abraham, but the eternal Word is before *all things*. Augustine writes, "Listen to it, or read it. But that's little enough, being the creator before Abraham; he's the creator before Adam, creator before heaven and earth, before all the angels, and the whole spiritual creation, 'thrones, dominions, principalities, and powers,' creator before all things whatsoever."[13]

The Arian belief that the Son is created or made makes no sense to Augustine, especially in light of John's gospel. "How can it happen that the Word of God was made when God made all things through the Word?"[14] Augustine rightly concludes that the creator cannot himself be created or made. "And if he was not made, then he is not a creature; but if he is not a creature, then he is the same substance with the Father . . . And if the Son is not of the same substance with the Father, then he is a substance that was made, then all things were not made by him; but 'all things were made by him' (*Jn* 1:3), therefore he is of one and the same substance with the Father."[15]

---

13. Augustine, *Sermons* 290.2; ACCS NT 9.16.
14. Augustine, *Tractates on the Gospel of John* 1,11,1; ACCS NT IVa, *John 1-10*, edited by Joel C. Elowsky (Downers Grove: InterVarsity Press, 2006), 20.
15. Augustine, *On the Trinity* 1.6 [9]; ACCS NT 4a.20.

* * *

Pause and reflect: Ponder prayerfully what Augustine is teaching. Allow his words to embed themselves in your mind and heart as you worship Jesus. The eternal Word is uncreated. He is not made by anyone or anything. He is not a creature. He shares the same "substance" with the Father. If he did not share the same substance, he would necessarily be "made", a creature. The Scripture is crystal clear, Augustine teaches. " '. . . all things were made by him' (*Jn* 1:3), therefore he is of one and the same substance with the Father."[16] What response do you sense the Lord is calling you to make to these wonders and beauties? Write down carefully what comes to mind.

* * *

Cyril of Alexandria, archbishop in Alexandria during Augustine's later years, like Augustine emphasizes that the Son is not a creature. Cyril points to the same words in John's gospel that had caught Augustine's eye. "The fact that all things 'were made through him,' will not, I think, cause any damage concerning what is said about the Son. For the Son is not introduced here as an employee or servant of someone else's will just because it says that the things that exist were made *through* him."[17] Nor is the Son "given the power of creation by someone else." No. The Son "being alone the strength of God the Father, as Son, as only begotten, he works all things, the Father and the Holy Spirit co-working and coexisting with him. For all things are from the Father through the Son in the Holy Spirit."[18]

Athanasius offers further insights. The eternal Word as the agent of creation reflects the order we have already seen within the Holy Trinity. Athanasius is quick to observe that the Word was not a creation of the Father designed to serve as maker of "all things." No, even if God had determined never to create anything, his Word would still be present with him, for the Word is eternal, as God is eternal. "For even if God had

---

16. Ibid.
17. Cyril of Alexandria, *Commentary on the Gospel of John* 1.5; ACCS NT: 4a, 20.
18. Ibid.

decided not to make created things, still the Word would have nonetheless been 'with God' and the Father in him."[19]

Still, since God has willed to create, he does so through his Word. Once again the analogy of the sun and its rays is helpful. "As the light enlightens all things with its radiance, and without that radiance nothing would be illuminated, so the Father wrought all things through the Word, as by a hand." Why through the Word? ". . . the Word of God is creator and maker, and he is the Father's very will."[20]

Let's summarize what Athanasius has taught us so far in this book:

- The relationship between the Son and the Father is absolutely unique. Nothing in creation corresponds to it.
- The Father has always been Father.
- The Son has always been Son.
- The relationship between the Father and the Son is eternal, not temporal.
- An eternal Father must have an eternal Son.
- The Father begets the Son.
- The Son is begotten by the Father.
- The Father and the Son are relationally distinct as persons.
- The Father and Son share the same substance or essence.
- Beware of theological pride and presumption.

My mind is drawn to an African proverb as I think about Athanasius and other African fathers. "When there is a big tree, small ones climb on its back to reach the sun." Little trees that we are, let's continue to climb the big ones!

---

19. Athanasius, *Against the Arians* 2.31; ACD 2.77.
20. Ibid.

6

FOR US

For us and for our salvation he came down from heaven...

Many readers of this book are African or African-American. Have you experienced hatred and persecution because of your Christian beliefs? Such was often the experience of African Christians in the early centuries of the church's history. Let's repeat an exercise from earlier in this book.

Try to name specific instances where you were called to confess your faith and paid a price for doing so. Perhaps note them in a journal. What age were you? Were you a new Christian? Or a more experienced believer? What happened? Were your persecutors known to you? Why do you think they were so resistant to your life or message? Were they angry with your words, or your life? What was the price you paid for your faithfulness?

We've seen so far that African church fathers played a key role in the formulation of the Nicene Creed. Once again I encourage you to get to know them well. As you do so, continue to pause and reflect on the following questions. I've asked them before:

Who are the Christian leaders who have significantly influenced your thinking and your life? Try listing them. Have they had a positive or negative effect? How so? List African or African-American leaders who have affected you. If you find your experience of African or African-American wisdom is limited, what specific steps can you take to broaden your knowledge base?

African issues and struggles in the ancient church are still pertinent for us today. The insights of the African fathers can help us as we navigate our present questions, concerns, problems, and context. Sometimes they express insights their ancient African environment engendered that are surprisingly helpful to us in our modern world. White Europeans and North Americans, along with Hispanic and Asian folks, can learn much from these ancient Christian ancestors. Work at creating mental space for them to occupy in your present environment.

* * *

Pause and Reflect: List three questions, issues, or problems you are currently facing in your own particular life setting. Then, when an African father's insights seem relevant, be sure to note them. You might write the church father's insight into your journal or note it in a file on your computer. Occasionally review these insights as you collect them.

* * *

We are now prepared to consider the first two words of our next key phrase: **"For us and for our salvation he came down from heaven..."**

"FOR US"

The eternal Son of God, one with the Father and the Holy Spirit, became incarnate **for us**. God, in the person of the Son, became a human being, while simultaneously remaining God.

Why would God -- the Holy Trinity -- do such a thing? God acted on our behalf because God loves his human image-bearers with a boundless, eternal love, a love that has neither beginning nor end. Divine love's embodiment in Jesus Christ wiggles its toes in a feeding trough in Bethlehem. The Son of God enters our world with a specific goal in mind: to save human beings from what we have become in our sin, and to heal our human nature.

What happened to "us" that required such a profound and surprising action on God's part, such a radical rescue operation? When Adam and Eve freely and willfully sinned, the contagion of sin and evil contaminated the world and us. Their disobedience released a corruption that infested human nature. From that point on, human nature was no longer what God created it to be.

Human nature continues to manifest a decidedly self-centered bias and bent. Martin Luther describes human nature after the Fall of Adam and Eve with a lively Latin expression – it is now *incurvatus in se* – *curved in on itself*. We are bent creatures, curved in on ourselves away from God. Luther borrowed this idea and phrase from Augustine, and it describes well an African perspective on the consequence of Adam and Eve's sin.

Every human being has repeated the sin of our original parents. Like Adam and Eve, we sinfully choose to place the self -- the ego --at the center of our lives. This is the default position for the fallen human ego. "Meet my needs," we demand. "I may be listening to you, but I'm thinking about me."

For the African fathers, sin and sinning involves a corrupting event and process initiated with our conception. This illness is terminal. The great African bishop Athanasius constantly refers to the corruption – the rot -- that permeates human nature; we are decaying on our feet. We are indeed the living dead. If we glimpsed our genuine condition in the mirror, we'd run screaming into the night.

Things were not always this way. Athanasius reminds us that God graciously provided Adam and Eve with their "own paradise, he gave then a law, so that if they guarded the grace and remained good, they might have the life of paradise – without sorrow, pain, or care – besides the promise of their incorruptibility in heaven."[1]

Sadly, our ancient parents freely chose to disobey God, choosing to trust in the devil's lie, and their human nature instantaneously curved inward away from God. They became bent creatures, like you and me. Now "they would know themselves enduring the corruption of death according to nature, and no longer live in paradise, but thereafter dying outside of it, and would remain in death and corruption."[2]

---

1. St. Athanasius the Great of Alexandria, *On the Incarnation*, Preface by C.S. Lewis, Translation and Introduction by John Behr (Yonkers, New York: St Vladimir's Seminary Press, 2011), 52.
2. Ibid.

* * *

Pause and Reflect: How does your corrupt bentness demonstrate itself in your thinking? In your living? How does this human self-centeredness manifest itself in your family, and your culture? Try to be as honest as possible. For your eyes only, unless you feel led to share with others.

* * *

GOD'S RESPONSE

So, how did God respond to this horrible turn of events? Augustine explores the dynamics of God's gracious plan to save. Ponder the following quotation from Augustine.

"When sins had made *a wide rift* between humanity and God, it *was necessary* that we should be *reconciled* to God and even *brought to the resurrection to eternal life by means of a mediator* who *alone was without sin in his birth, life and execution*, so that *humankind's pride should be shown up and cured by the humility of God.*"[3]

Now let's divide the quotation into manageable parts:

- Our sins "made a wide rift between humanity and God."
- This rift made it "necessary" that we "be reconciled to God."
- Hence, the need for a "mediator" who through the resurrection would bring us to eternal life.
- This mediator "alone was without sin in his birth, life, and execution."
- Our horrific pride was "cured by the humility of God."

In the same passage, Augustine continues: "Humanity is thus shown how *far it had departed from God* since it was through the God-man that an example of obedience was offered to the insolence of humankind. And so *a fountain of grace* was opened, not for any antecedent merit, but *by the taking of 'the form of a servant' (Phil. 2:7) by the Only-Begotten.*"[4]

---

3. Augustine, *Enchiridion* 108; ACD 2.94; my emphasis.
4. Ibid., my emphasis.

- God's healing acts to save demonstrate how far human beings "had departed from God."
- The incarnate "God-man" offered the example of obedience to "the insolence of humankind." The Son of God desires for us to see what Christ's obedience looks like. It is a "fountain of grace" demonstrated by the "only begotten" Son "taking the form 'of a servant.'" Philippians 2: 7 is an extremely important text for the African fathers and will frequently appear in their reflections.

Augustine resumes:

Proof of the bodily resurrection promised to the redeemed was given by anticipation in the person of the Redeemer himself. The devil was overcome by means of that very nature that, he rejoiced to think, he had entrapped. Yet humankind should not boast, lest pride should arise again. And there are other consequences of this mighty and mysterious work of the mediator that can be seen and described by those who benefit from it, or can be seen, though they cannot be described.[5]

- Proof of Jesus' resurrection was promised "to the redeemed" and "given by anticipation" in the person of Jesus himself.
- The devil, the great deceiver, was "overcome" by the very human nature that he thought he "had entrapped."
- Humans should never "boast", lest "pride should rise again."
- Augustine teaches that these saving acts of God demonstrate what God's surprising and gracious humility has done for us and the consequences "can be seen and described by those who benefit from it."
- Other aspects of Christ the mediator's work "can be seen, though they cannot be described."

* * *

Pause and Reflect: Ponder slowly what Augustine has written in these three passages we have read from the *Enchiridion*. Are there one or two

---
5. Ibid., 94-95.

statements that you sense are especially applicable to you and your life experiences? If so, write them down and return to them in the future. They are gifts from Augustine, who is still alive and well today in heaven. Perhaps God had you especially in mind as the Holy Spirit guided Augustine as he was writing.

There are hidden depths to the African fathers' writing that are not immediately perceived by us if we move too quickly through their words. Pace yourself. Don't hurry. There is a reason why these fathers are still in print. Now let's return to Athanasius, whose thought on human nature's corruption through sin we briefly considered.

* * *

WE WERE THE OCCASION OF CHRIST'S EMBODIMENT

Athanasius observes that human beings freely choose to sin, and therefore stand guilty before God. We are embodied creatures, possess free will, and have freely chosen to disobey God. No one forced us to do so. Yet where sin occurs, the grace of God is always present and accessible to faith. In the incarnation, Athanasius teaches, God in the person of the Son became embodied on our behalf.

God does not abandon us because of our sin, though he could have chosen to do so. No, in great love God acts to heal human nature and responds to our genuine guilt with undeserved kindness. "*Our guilt was the cause of the descent of the Word, and our transgression called forth his loving kindness,* so that he came to us, and the Lord was displayed among human beings. *For we were the occasion of his embodiment,* and for our salvation he went so far in his love for humankind as to be born and to be displayed in a human body."[6]

* * *

Pause and Reflect: This is a wonderful passage from Athanasius's great work *On the Incarnation*; read it slowly. Pop it in your mouth like a candy lozenge and enjoy its sweetness. God does not waver in his love for

---

6. Athanasius, *On the Incarnation* 4; ACD 2.88; my emphasis.

human beings. Nor does God ignore our sin and guilt. Rather, God's reaction to the horror story of Adam and Eve's sin – a story we have retold and recapitulated in the narrative of our own lives -- is unexpected and undeserved kindness. How do you sense God is specifically calling you to respond to the Son's embodiment on your behalf?

* * *

God the Son comes to us -- endowed with all that characterizes human nature apart from sin -- to heal and restore.

"God," as James Martin writes, "meets us where we are. . . God comes to us in ways that we can understand and appreciate. . . God could have come to the world in any way that God desired. We may be so conditioned to the story of the birth of Jesus in humble circumstances that we forget that this was a choice. God could have come to us as a powerful ruler, born into a family of wealth and privilege. . . But God wanted to meet us where we are. So God came, first of all, as a human being, as something – someone – other men and women could approach. God is not only a flaming bush, a pillar of fire, or even a mysterious cloud, as God is described in various places in the Old Testament. God is one of us."[7]

Cyril of Alexandria echoes Athanasius's words on the Son's compassion in descending to save us. In the saving, Jesus confers unexpected benefits and beauties. "The Lord of the universe, the only-begotten God, submitted himself to deprivation for our sakes, so that he might generously confer on us the privilege of brotherhood with him, and the beauty, all to be desired, of his own inherent nobility."[8]

The Son submits to "deprivation" for our sakes with a very specific goal in mind, to bestow on us the honor of brotherhood with him. Not only are we considered brothers and sisters of Jesus; we are awarded the status of nobility. Do we deserve this honor? The answer is self-evident. Simply ask yourself how you've behaved over the last week or month. Never ask God for what you deserve. Instead, humbly ask for grace and mercy. God will gladly respond.

---

7. James Martin, SJ, *Jesus: A Pilgrimage* (San Francisco: HarperOne, 2014), 64.
8. Cyril of Alexandria, *Against Nestorius* 3.2; ACD 2.89.

From the perspective of the church fathers, salvation entails more than atonement, though it surely includes this. What is the "more" they celebrate? *It is the healing of human nature itself.* It is the reversal and eradication of corruption. It is the communication of life, the life of the resurrected Son of God. Tuck away these thoughts in your mind and heart.

Let's direct our attention to a few other ancient Christian writers who capture well the dynamics of the incarnation; the Son entered the world as the Nicene Creed states, "for us and for our salvation."

The Epistle of Barnabas, written between 70 and 132 CE, captures the loving paradox of the incarnation. "The Son of God, although he is Lord and Judge of the living and the dead, underwent suffering, so that his affliction might give us life."[9] The Son of God, though he is rightly the Lord and Judge of the living and the dead, willingly suffers on our behalf. Through his suffering, Jesus gives us life. Later church fathers will develop this fundamental theme in great depth.

Basil the Great, for instance, writes that ". . . for your sake he became dead." Why? ". . . to free you from mortality and make you partake of the heavenly life."[10] Mortality characterized Jesus's body, for he was able to die and became subject to death for our sake. The risen Christ, though, is immortal. Indeed, those joined to him will one day be immortal as he is, incapable of dying and filled with the divine life.

Ancient heretics mocked the possibility of God becoming a human being. The followers of Arius were chief among them. As John McGuckin comments, "Arian apologists" – those who defended Arius's ideas – "mocked the Nicene belief that Jesus was personally and directly the incarnate Word, on the grounds that the human fallibilities and passibilities demonstrated in the earthly life (the sufferings and death on the cross in particular) were wholly unfitting for the impassible Logos."[11] God would surely not act or respond to us in this way.

Basil replies that this is exactly how God would act. "It is just as if one should find fault with a physician for bending down to sickness and breathing its stench, in order that he may heal the sufferers."[12] Gregory of

---

9. *Epistle of Barnabas* 7.1-2; ACD 2.80.
10. Basil of Caesarea, *Letter* 8.5; ACD 2.81.
11. ACD 2.81.
12. Basil of Caesarea, *Letter 8.5*, op. cit; ACD 2.81.

Nyssa also describes the incarnate Son of God as a physician who comes to perform critical and painful surgery.[13]

Robert Sarah, an African church leader, comments on the Son's willingness to enter and identify with our misery: "He is not content to descend into the deep waters of the Jordan. Christ descends also to the very depths of human misery, to the regions of broken hearts and ruined relationships, to the most depraved carnal dictatorships and the desolate places of a world marred by sin."[14]

We all know that patients don't always appreciate the healing hands of a surgeon, for surgeons hurt to heal. We allow a surgeon to operate because we trust in his knowledge and skill. "Those who submit to surgery or cautery are angry with their doctors as they smart under the agony of the operation. But if restoration to health follows and the pain passes, they are grateful to those who effected the cure."[15]

* * *

Pause and Reflect: Have there been times when you have resisted God's surgery? Why? What was the result of your resistance? Try to be as specific as possible in your response.

* * *

The African bishop Cyprian honestly acknowledged his need for deep healing and second birth. He indeed suffered from the "stench" Basil later wrote about, and at one time doubted that real transformation could occur in his life. Carefully consider Cyprian's personal testimony, worth reflecting on at length:

> While I was still lying in darkness and gloomy night, tossed about on the foam of this boastful age, and uncertain of my wandering steps, knowing nothing of my real life, and remote from truth and light, I used to regard it

---

13. Gregory of Nyssa, *Address on Religious Instruction* 26; ACD 2.81.
14. Robert Cardinal Sarah, with Nicolas Diat, *The Power of Silence: Against the Dictatorship of Noise*, with an Afterword by Pope Emeritus Benedict XVI, translated by Michael J. Miller (San Francisco: Ignatius Press, 2017), 64.
15. Gregory of Nyssa, *Address on Religious Instruction* 26; ACD 2.81.

as a difficult matter, and especially as difficult in respect of my character at that time, that a man should be capable of being born again . . . These were my frequent thoughts. For I was held in bonds by the innumerable errors of my previous life, from which I did not believe I could possibly be delivered . . .[16]

* * *

Pause and Reflect: Can you identify with Cyprian's struggle? Have "innumerable errors" in your own life distanced you from God? How encouraging to know that even great African bishops mightily struggled before they entered the kingdom of God -- and after. Try to identify three points of struggle where you continue to doubt you can actually change.

* * *

PARADOXICAL HEALING

This intimate movement of the eternal Son into union with human nature is replete with paradoxes. Should we be surprised? John R. Betz describes well how paradox often protects mysteries of God such as the incarnation. ". . .let us recall that, in Christianity, paradoxes are often like veils before the mysteries or, better, like gargoyles guarding them from profane minds who refuse to be led by faith to something deeper than they can imagine."[17] Arius is a fine example of Betz's point.

Gregory of Nazianzus captures well the paradoxical nature of the incarnation:

What he was, he continued to be. What he was not, he took to himself. In the beginning he was uncaused; for what is the cause of God? But afterward for a cause he was born. And that cause was that you might be saved . . . He was born, but he had been begotten. He was born of a woman, but

---

16. Cyprian, *Letter to Donatus;* quoted in Robert Cardinal Sarah, op. cit., 66-67.
17. John R. Betz, "The Analogy of Tradition: Toward a More Radical Ressourcement," *The New Ressourcement,* Vol. 1, No. 3, Fall 2024, 525.

she was a virgin. The first is human; the second, divine. In his human nature he had no father, but also in his divine nature, no mother.[18]

The Son of God assumes human nature to heal and cleanse it, to restore it to what God had initially created us to be. Take time to ponder Gregory of Nyssa's words:

> When after tedious processes the evil is expelled that had been mixed with human nature and had grown up with it, and when there has occurred the restoration to the original state of those who are now lying in wickedness, then will arise a unison of thanksgiving from all creatures . . . Such are the benefits conferred by the great mystery of the divine incarnation. . . . For the purification of the disease, however painful, is the healing of infirmity.[19]

Gregory, like many of the African fathers, focuses on the healing communicated to human nature as it is joined to the Son's divine nature in the incarnation. "For the purification of the disease, however painful, is the healing of infirmity."[20]

This healing is painful for the incarnate Son because of what it requires: human birth, growing up in a small town in Nazareth, ministry to apostles who rarely understand what Jesus is saying and doing, rejection by the very people he had come to save, suffering in Gethsemane, trial and conviction on false testimony before the Sanhedrin, and crucifixion by the Roman government. By all appearances everything has gone wrong, yet all things were actually being made right.

Consider the healing process Christ introduces to human nature: the Son of God assumes all that we are apart from sin in the incarnation. He possesses a genuine human mind, body, soul, and will. Everything that constitutes human nature is assumed by the Son. Then, because Christ's human nature is joined to his divine nature in the incarnation, it benefits from all the divine nature offers to it in this ineffable, wondrous union.

The incarnation of the Son of God is an utterly unique event in human

---

18. Gregory of Nazianzus, *Oration* 29.19; ACD 2.81.
19. Gregory of Nyssa, *Address on Religious Instruction*, 26; ACD 2.81. I have slightly modified the bumpy translation.
20. Ibid.

history. Tertullian, though, reminds us that Christ's birth is not the first time the Son of God appeared, for he had occasionally acted in the history of Israel. For instance, Tertullian writes, the Son conversed with Adam, appeared or spoke "to the patriarchs and prophets", as he sometimes revealed himself in visions and dreams "as in an enigma."[21]

Tertullian comments that the Old Testament appearances or theophanies helped "prepare the way of faith for us, to make it easier for us to believe that the Son of God has descended into the temporal world, seeing that we know that something of the kind had been done in times past."[22]

* * *

Pause and Reflect: Thank God for the generosity displayed in the Son of God's breathtaking humility, poverty, patience, and love. Athanasius accentuates these themes in his comments on the incarnation.

> The Son of God assumed human nature, and in it he endured all that belongs to the human condition. This is a remedy for humankind of a power beyond our imagining. Could any pride be cured, if the humility of God's Son does not cure it? Could any greed be cured, if the poverty of God's Son does not cure it? Or any anger, if the patience of God's Son does not cure it? Or any coldness, if the love of God's Son does not cure it? Lastly, what fearfulness can be cured if it is not cured by the resurrection of the body of Christ the Lord?[23]

Carefully consider Athanasius's comparisons: our pride with Christ's humility. Our greed with Christ's poverty. Our anger with Jesus' patience. Our cold disposition with the warmth of the Son's love. Our wide ranging fearfulness cured by the resurrection of Jesus from the dead.

Did you notice the verb that Athanasius repeats throughout this passage? In the English text various forms of "cure" occur eight times. *Athanasius is making a very important point. The Son of God in the incarnation is healing human nature. He is curing our grave illness.*

---

21. Tertullian, *Against Praxeas* 16; ACD 2.81-82.
22. Ibid.
23. Athanasius, *On the Agony of Christ* 12; ACD 2.82.

Picture the Son's divine nature – with all its benefits -- radiating into our corrupt, cancerous human nature. God the Son is not killing human nature, for he created it, loves it, and is now restoring it. Indeed, he is recreating it to its glorious state in Eden before the Fall. Athanasius longs for us to recognize how elevated, how wondrous, how beautiful divinely healed human nature is.

> Let humankind raise its hopes and recognize its own nature. Let it observe how high a place it has in the works of God. Do not despise yourselves, you humans: the Son of God assumed humanity. Do not despise yourselves, you women: God's Son was born of a woman.[24]

Ponder the opposite of "despise." If we are not to despise human nature, how should we respond? I found the following antonyms for despise:

- Accept.
- Admire.
- Adore.
- Cherish.
- Like.
- Love.
- Praise.
- Approve.
- Respect.

Athanasius encourages us as God's precious image-bearers to use words such as these to reflect on the wonder and glory of redeemed human nature. This clarified vision and understanding of who we are, Athanasius believes, should significantly affect our attitudes, habits, perspectives, choices, and behavior. The patterns apparent in the incarnation are important to notice and remember.

* * *

---

24. Ibid.

> But do not set your hearts on the satisfactions of the body, for in the Son of God we are 'neither male nor female' (*Gal* 3:28). Do not set your heart on temporal rewards, for if it were good to do so, that human nature that God's Son assumed would have thus set its heart. Do not fear insults, crosses and death, for if they did humanity harm, then the humanity that God's Son assumed would not have endured them.[25]

The values and perspectives Athanasius advocates are pointedly different from those fallen human beings habitually pursue. For instance, Athanasius wonders why anyone would set his heart "on temporal rewards."[26] Christ's attitudes and behaviors illustrate the divine pattern for redeemed, restored human nature. For Jesus' incarnation and resurrection has healed human nature, and Christ invites us to experience this healing.

The restoration of human nature to its original blueprint has been accomplished by Father, Son, and Holy Spirit **"for us"**. The holy Trinity was of one mind that the incarnation and its attendant glories should occur.

---

25. Ibid.
26. Ibid.

7
OUR SALVATION

. . . and for our salvation, he came down from heaven. . .

*W*hy does this first phrase – "and for our salvation" – occur in the Nicene Creed? Why the necessity to state this, which seems a no-brainer for modern Christians?

Recall that much of the Nicene Creed was written against the background of Arianism. Arius argued that Jesus was a creature -- elevated above all other creatures -- but a creature, nonetheless. If so, the Son of God did not enter the world to save us from our sin. If only a creature, he could not do so. What, then, did Jesus come to do? All Arius could offer was Jesus as *an example* of how human beings should live.

So, in light of this Arian background to the formation of the Nicene Creed, it becomes plain why "and for our salvation" is so important. The Son of God *came to save*, not merely to serve as an example of how to live. The question then becomes, how does he do so? Let's consider for a moment the thought of the great African Augustine.

Augustine sees an exchange taking place, unexpected and amazing. God the Son becomes a human being, enabling human beings to participate in Christ's divinity; all this begins with the birth of a baby.

A baby? God demonstrates his "generosity" and "moral power" in just such a move. "That moral power, without changing for the worse, took to itself the rational soul, and through that the human body, and the whole man, to change it for the better; in condescension taking from it the name of humanity, in generosity bestowing on it the name of divinity."[1]

Irenaeus, writing years before Augustine in the second century CE, had made much the same point. "Our Lord Jesus Christ, the Word of God, of his boundless love, became what we are that he might make us what he himself is."[2]

Athanasius makes a number of comments worthy of our careful consideration:

- *"The Word was made man in order that we might be made divine.* He displayed himself through a body that we might receive knowledge of the invisible Father. He endured insults at the hands of people that we might inherit immortality.[3]

- "For when the Word was made man he did not cease to be God, nor because he is God does he avoid what is human. Far from it; *rather, being God, he has taken the flesh to himself, and, in flesh, deified the flesh.* In the flesh he asked questions; in the flesh he raised the dead. He knew where Lazarus lay, but he still asked . . . The all-holy Word of God bore our ignorance so that he might bestow on us the knowledge of his Father."[4]

- "If the works of the Godhead had not taken place by means of the body, humankind would not have been made divine. If the properties of the flesh had not been ascribed to the Word, humans would not have been thoroughly freed from them. But as it is the Word became man and took as his own the properties of the flesh."[5]

Let's summarize what Athanasius has written:

---

1. Augustine, *Letter* 137.8; ACD 2.90.
2. Irenaeus, *Against Heresies* 5.Preface; ACD 2.91.
3. Athanasius, *On the Incarnation* 54; ACD 2.91; my emphasis.
4. Athanasius, *Against the Arians* 3.38; ACD 2.92; my emphasis.
5. Ibid., 3.33; ACD 2.92.

- God had a specific purpose in mind when the Son of God became human and assumed a human body.

- This purpose was that we "might be made divine." Now, we will always remain human creatures. Athanasius isn't saying that we will become God like God is God. Athanasius does affirm, however, that God in Christ is inviting us to participate in Christ's deity, and believes that this participation was God's original plan for human beings (cf. 2 *Pet* 1:4).

- Jesus had a human body through which we "might receive knowledge of the invisible Father." Think of Jesus' words to Philip in John 14:9. "He who has seen me has seen the Father."

- Jesus suffered in his body, enduring "insults at the hands of people that we might inherit immortality."

- When the Word (cf. *Jn* 1:1) became a man and took on flesh (*Jn* 1:14), he did not cease to be God.

- As God, the Son took the flesh of his humanity and deified it.

- The union between Christ's deity and humanity is mysterious and doesn't fit into our logical categories. It is incomprehensible. For instance, as a human being Jesus asked where Lazarus was buried, while as God he knew full well the answer to his question. When we look at Jesus and listen to him, at times we will discern his humanity, and at other times his deity.

"...HE CAME DOWN FROM HEAVEN..."

Our next clause states that "he came down." African writers frequently commented on John 1:1. In this text John affirms the preexistence of the Word, that the Word was with God, and that the Word was God. Not only so, but John's first chapter declares a wondrous, unexpected truth. The eternal Word has become a human being. "The Word became flesh and made his dwelling among us. We have seen his glory, the glory of the one and only Son, who came from the Father, full of grace and truth" (*Jn* 1:14).

Few, if any, expected that God would or could become incarnate, nor that there was this marvelously strange relational complexity within the very being of God that the incarnation demonstrates.

Tertullian was one of the earliest African writers to capture the wonder of the incarnation. The eternal Son had entered our world by descending from heaven to be born of the virgin Mary.

Here, wriggling in a feeding trough in Bethlehem, was a human male baby who was both human and God. In Tertullian's work *On the Flesh of Christ*, we encounter a gifted theologian plumbing the depths of these two simultaneous truths: God was now fully human in the person of the incarnate Son, while never ceasing to be fully God.

"Was not God really crucified? Did he not really die after real crucifixion? Did he not really rise again, after real death?"[6] Tertullian perceived that the Christian faith depended upon such strange paradoxes. Crucifixion, death, and burial seemed entirely unworthy of God. Even shameful. Yet "all that is unworthy of God is for my benefit . . . The Son of God was born: shameful, therefore there is no shame. The Son of God died: absurd, and therefore utterly credible. He was buried and rose again: impossible, and therefore a fact."[7]

On the one hand, Tertullian is shocked that the eternal Son has become incarnate. On the other, he knows that the basics of the gospel affirm this to be true. Christ has come. Christ has died. Christ has been buried. Christ is raised from the dead. Christ will come again. Each statement affirms that the eternal Son has come down "from heaven" on our behalf.

The incarnation reveals "the two modes of being . . . the humanity and the divinity: born as man, unborn as God; in one respect carnal, in the other spiritual; in one respect weak, in the other exceedingly strong; in one respect dying, in the other living." Each nature displays, Tertullian writes, "the proper qualities of the two conditions, the divine and the human."[8]

---

6. Tertullian, *On the Flesh of Christ* 5; ACD 2:110
7. Ibid.
8. Ibid.

We struggle to understand how God can remain fully God while becoming a human being. Yet when we gaze upon the beauty of the incarnate Son, we affirm he is both omniscient in his deity, and growing in knowledge in his humanity. Consider my paraphrase of Ephraim the Syrian's poetry: "He who knows all things begins to learn. He who occupies all space lies in a manger." Both are true of the incarnate Son, who has come down from heaven to save us. And both must be true if we are to be saved.

* * *

Pause and Reflect: Take a piece of paper and draw a line down the middle. Label the left column "human characteristics." List every characteristic of a human male. Don't list characteristics true of sinful humans, such as vices. For instance, all humans occasionally experience greed, envy, or lust. Jesus didn't, for he never sinned.

Now, in the right hand column list "characteristics of God." List whatever you believe the Bible teaches is true of God. An example would be omniscience; God knows all that is possible to know. When you have finished your list, compare the columns. Tertullian teaches that both columns are true of Jesus. The Nicene Creed does, too.

How this could be true is beyond human comprehension. The church affirms the incomprehensibility of the incarnation, for we simply don't understand how both columns can be true of Jesus. Yet they are. Occasionally, prayerfully ponder what you've written.

* * *

The African exegete Origen captures the incarnate mystery well. ". . . the Word that 'was in the beginning with God and was himself God' (Jn 1:1) comes to us; yet he does not leave his home or desert his state."[9]

When the eternal Word came down "from heaven," what happened? Did he leave heaven in the sense that he was no longer there after his coming to earth? No. Such could not be the case if the incarnate Word is God, for God is fully present in all places.

The incarnation was not the change of God into a human being, with

---

9. Origen, *Against Celsus* 4 5; ACD 2:111.

divinity now left behind. Rather, it was the unexpected, grace-filled union of the divine nature of the Son with the human nature freely offered to him by the Virgin Mary.

As the Nicene Creed states, the Son became incarnate "for us and for our salvation." In the incarnation God the Son enters into union with human nature. Origen puts it this way: The Word "became for the benefit of mortal people, becoming, that is, for them what each of them needed to become..."[10]

What a beautiful thought. The Son of God lovingly enters our world, becomes all that we are apart from sin, joins our human nature to his divine nature, all so that each of us could become what we were originally created to be. And, of course, at the heart of this redemptive movement is Christ's crucifixion and resurrection. He lived in a human body and died in a human body. He rose in a human body. He ascended into heaven in a human body, though the nature of that body had been transformed (1 *Cor* 15:35-57).

Athanasius delights in these great incarnational themes. The Apostle John writes that "the Word became flesh" (*Jn* 1:14). If this is true, Athanasius believes, "then resurrection and exaltation must be ascribed to him, in respect of his manhood, that the death ascribed to him may be a redemption for the sins of humans and an annihilation of death and that the resurrection and exaltation may because of him be kept secure for us."[11]

Christ has healed human nature through its participation in his divine nature. The apostle Peter refers to this wonder in his second letter. "Through these he has given us his very great and precious promises, so that through them you many participate in the divine nature, having escaped the corruption in the world caused by evil desires." (2 *Pet* 1:4, NIV). This was a favorite text of Athanasius.

In the incarnate Son, deity and humanity join in an ineffable, incomprehensible union and in Christ we gracefully receive the benefits of this union. Who knew that God could do such a wonder? Our great healing and saving have begun in Christ, rooted in the wonder of the incarnation.

Our human nature will remain in union with the ascended Jesus for all eternity, for the divine Son will never cease being human, nor divine. This

---

10. Origen, *Commentary on the Gospel of Matthew* 15.24; ACD 2.112.
11. Athanasius, *Against the Arians* 1.45; ACD 2.112.

was decided once and for at Bethlehem. Jesus, the God-Man, has ascended and now sits at the right hand of the Father, with human nature healed, raised, transformed, and exalted in Christ.

The incarnation establishes for us secure truths, because Christ has risen from the dead and ascended to the Father. Listen carefully again to Athanasius. He points to Paul's words in Ephesian 4:9 that speak of Christ's descent "to the lower, earthly regions." "He who descended," Paul writes, "is the very one who ascended higher than all the heavens, in order to fill the whole universe" (*Eph* 4:10). Jesus could descend because he had died in his body, just as he ascended in his resurrected body. "Both events are spoken of as his," Athanasius writes, "since it was his body, and not another's, that was exalted from the dead and taken up into heaven."[12]

The eternal Word's body was not "external" to the Word, as some Arians argued, but the very body of the divine Word (*Jn* 1:1, *Jn* 1:14). In the incarnation, the eternal Word communicates life – resurrected life -- to the body he has assumed. After the resurrection, Jesus then ascends to the Father, elevating human nature with him. "Again, since the body was his body, and since the Word was not external to it, it is natural that on the exaltation of his body, he, *as man*, should be said to be exalted on account of the body."[13]

Why is Athanasius pressing this point? The incarnation of the Son demonstrates that "the Word became flesh" (*Jn* 1:14), the very truth denied by the Arians. The Son's body was genuinely his body, for he – the eternal Son – had "become flesh," while remaining God. So, Athanasius rightly insists, "then resurrection and exaltation must be ascribed to him, *in respect of his manhood*, that the death ascribed to him may be a redemption of the sins of humans and an annihilation of death and that the resurrection and exaltation may because of him kept secure for us."[14]

* * *

Pause and Reflect: Consider memorizing the contours of Athanasius' argument. In the incarnation, the Son of God and eternal Word comes to

---

12. Ibid.
13. Ibid; my emphasis.
14. Ibid; my emphasis.

us from heaven. "He who is the Son of God himself became the Son of man. As the Word, he gives from the Father, for all that the Father does and gives he too does and supplies through him."[15] Of course he does, for he is fully divine, the Son of the Father, and fully human.

*   *   *

Now pay attention carefully to Athanasius's next step: the Son "gives" or "supplies" from the Father to the human nature he now possesses as the Son of Man. As God, he supplies or gives to himself as fully human. In this incarnational movement, human nature itself is exalted. "As the Son of Man he himself is said, humanly, *to receive what proceeds from himself. For he received it according to the exaltation of human nature.*"[16] The Son as the divine Word supplies his divinity to his human nature.

In turn, joined to Jesus by faith and baptism, we ourselves are deified. We participate in Christ's divinity. The church fathers call this participation deification or *theosis* (Gk.). Christ communicates to our human nature what is true of his own humanity, a human nature that participates in Christ's deity.

To repeat, the Word came "from heaven" and returns to heaven. As he returns in the ascension, he does so in union with our human nature, now deified, as both Peter (2 *Pet* 1:4) and Athanasius teach. "This exaltation was its deification, an exaltation that the Word himself always had in respect of the Godhead and perfection that was his own as inherited from his Father."[17]

---

15. Ibid.
16. Ibid; my emphasis.
17. Ibid.

8
FROM HEAVEN

. . . from heaven.

With the descent of the Son of God from heaven, Tertullian comments, the Son "is seen, heard, approached." He is "the agent and servant of the Father."[1] As we have seen, the incarnate Son is both fully human and fully divine. In Tertullian's words, he *"combines in himself man and God; God in his works of power, man in his weaknesses, so that he may confer on humanity as much as he withdraws from divinity."*[2]

* * *

Pause and Reflect: The last clause of Tertullian's thought just quoted should bring a smile to your face. Ponder the incarnational dynamic Tertullian describes. The Son becomes what we are in our weakness, so that he can communicate to our weak and fragile human nature what "he withdraws" from his divine nature. Try to describe this dynamic in your own words.

* * *

---

1. Tertullian, *Against Marcion* 2.27; ACD 2.97.
2. Ibid; my emphasis.

Yes, in Christ we *participate* in the divine nature, a truth we just noted the apostle Peter refers to in his second letter. "His divine power has given us everything we need for a godly life through our knowledge of him who called us by his own glory and goodness. Through these he has given us his very great and precious promises, so that through them you may participate in the divine nature, having escaped the corruption in the world caused by evil desires" (2 *Pet* 1:3-4, NIV).

"In this way of thinking," Tertullian writes, "all that you see as my God's disgrace is really the mystery of human salvation. God lived with humanity, as man, that humanity might be taught to live the divine life. God lived on humanity's level that humanity might be able to live on God's level. God was found weak that humanity might become most great. If you disdain a God like this, I doubt if you wholeheartedly believe in a God who was crucified."[3]

Clement of Alexandria comments that God "is the God of compassion, yearning to save humankind. The Word himself at this point speaks to you plainly, putting unbelief to shame, and I mean the Word of God, *who became man just that you may learn from a man how it may be that Man should become God.*"[4] In Clement we again encounter the theme of participation in the divine nature. We don't change into God, leaving our humanity behind. Rather, we participate in God and our human nature is radiated with the Son's divine nature.

Athanasius believes Paul's words in Philippians 2:9 are relevant to our understanding of deification. The incarnate Son has been given a "name above all names." This is a new name, for as the eternal Word he was "already worshiped by the angels and by the whole creation in respect of his unique heritage."[5] Now, as the eternal Word enters our world to save us as the incarnate Christ, he receives what he has always possessed as God, "in order that this great gift might extend to us. The Word was not degraded by receiving a body, so that he should ever need to seek to receive God's gift. Rather, *he deified what he put on; and, more than that, he bestowed this gift on the human race.*"[6]

Cyril of Alexandria, a later bishop of the church in that great Egyptian

---

3. Ibid.
4. Clement of Alexandria, *Exhortation to the Greeks* 1.8. (4); ACD 2.97; my emphasis.
5. Athanasius, *Against the Arians* 1.42; ACD 2.98.
6. Ibid, my emphasis.

city, reinforces the thoughts of earlier African leaders. The Son "came down for our salvation and emptied himself out of his condescension, and became incarnate and was made man."[7] The Son received his flesh from Mary "and made it his own from the womb." In doing so, though, "He did not cast away what he was, but even in the assumption of flesh and blood, he remained what he was, namely, God in nature and truth."[8]

Occasionally, as Athanasius had earlier commented, Christ's human nature manifests its reality. For instance, Jesus says in Mark 13:32 that there are some things only the Father knows. If so, we rightly ask, how could the incarnate Son be fully divine?

Athanasius responds that "every believer knows the answer: that he spoke, as elsewhere, as man, because of the flesh. This does not show a defect in the Word but rather defect of human nature, of which ignorance is a characteristic. Since he was made man, he is not ashamed to profess ignorance because of the ignorance of flesh, to show that knowing as God he is ignorant according to the flesh."[9]

Do you get Athanasius's point? Jesus' human nature is limited in the extent of its knowledge, as is true of all human beings. However, remember that Jesus is also fully divine, and hence possesses infinite knowledge as God. Again we encounter the wonder and mystery of the incarnation. Some ancient Christians were tempted to reduce this paradoxical mystery by either saying that Jesus wasn't fully human, or wasn't fully God. In response, the church in the Nicene Creed insisted on preserving the mystery.

So, because Jesus is both divine and human, his knowledge as a human being is limited, and as God is boundless. Athanasius teaches that our awareness that the one person -- Jesus -- has two natures, enhances our ability to interpret the Bible well, for some texts reflect Jesus' infinite knowledge as God, and other texts highlight his limited understanding as a human being. Mark 13:32 would be one such text, where Jesus states that the time of the end "no one knows, not even the angels in heaven, nor the Son, but only the Father." There are some things only the Father

---

7. Cyril of Alexandria, *Third Letter to Nestorius* (Letter 17); ACD 2.99.
8. Ibid.
9. Athanasius, *Against the Arians* 3.43; ACD 2.100.

knows. The Son in his humanity doesn't know them. Yet his knowledge as God is identical with that of the Father and the Holy Spirit.

If you're scratching your head as to how Jesus can truly be both divine and human, you have entered the mystery the incarnation presents to us. The incarnation of the eternal Word is an incomprehensible revelation that can only be described and worshiped, but not understood. This incomprehensible wonder and beauty lies at the center of the Christian faith, and sheds light on every aspect of what Christians believe.

Cyril of Alexandria reminds us that in the incarnation Christ's human nature is not "converted into the divine nature," nor is the divine nature "debased and perverted into the nature of the flesh."[10] Why can't the divine nature be changed into the flesh? ". . . the nature of God is unchangeable and unalterable, ever continuing altogether the same, according to the Scriptures."[11] What, then, can we say without error? We affirm Christ's humanity – with all the characteristics of human nature apart from sin, while simultaneously affirming all that can and should be predicated of his deity.

Cyril puts it this way:

> We, however, say that the Son of God, while visible to the eyes, and a babe, and in swaddling clothes and still at the breast of his virgin Mother, nevertheless filled all creation as God and was seated with his Father. For the divinity is without quantity and without magnitude and without limit.[12]

Note Cyril's emphasis that God is "without quantity," "without magnitude," and "without limit." This is true because God's nature is infinite. God can't be subject to measurement of any kind because God has no limits, no boundaries. *He is boundless.* Tuck this away in your mind as a good definition of God's infinity. The incomprehensible mystery is that the God who has no boundaries whatever, lies wriggling in a manger!

Do you remember Paul's words in Philippians 2:9? "Therefore God exalted him to the highest place and gave him the name that is above every name." Athanasius writes that this exaltation is not the exaltation of

---

10. Cyril of Alexandria, *Third Letter to Nestorius* (Letter 17); ACD 2.100.
11. Ibid.
12. Ibid.

the eternal Word, who was, and is, and always will be eternally exalted. "When it says, 'God highly exalted him,' the words 'highly exalted' do not signify the exaltation of the substance of the Word; that was and is always equal with God." Rather, Paul is speaking of the exaltation "of the manhood" of Jesus, his human nature. "These words are said after the incarnation of the Word, to make it clear that the terms 'humbled' and 'exalted' refer to the human nature."[13]

The eternal Word, sent from the Father, comes to save, becoming a human male, while remaining the eternal Word. As a human being Christ suffers for us.

> ... he endured death for our sake in his own flesh, that thus he might offer himself to the Father on our behalf. Therefore also as man he is said to be highly exalted because of us and on our behalf, that as by his death we all died in Christ, so also in Christ himself we may all be exalted, being raised from the dead and ascending into heaven 'where Jesus the forerunner has entered for us' (*Heb* 6:20). And if it is now for our sake that Christ has entered into heaven, though he was before and always is the Lord and the maker of the heavens, it is therefore for our sake that the Scripture speaks of his being exalted.[14]

THE HUMILITY OF GOD

The church fathers emphasize *the humility of God* as the Word comes to us in a manner that we can perceive and yet not be overwhelmed. In the incarnation, Origen writes, God descends in a "size" that accommodates himself to us. God has no desire to overwhelm us. Rather, God wants to save us, and does so by becoming what we are, while remaining what God has always been. In the person of the Son, he comes as a human being to other humans.

Origen uses the example of a statue to make this point: "Let us suppose a statue of such a size as would fill the whole world, of such immensity that no one could contemplate it. Let us then suppose that another statue was made, identical with the first in respect of the shape of the limbs, the

---

13. Athanasius, *Against the Arians* 1.41; ACD 2.102.
14. Ibid.

features, the whole outward appearance and the material, like it in all respects apart from the immense size. This would be made for this purpose: that those who could not contemplate and behold the enormous statue might look at the small copy and claim that they had seen the original, insofar as the copy, being a complete likeness, preserved all the likeness of the limbs and the features, in fact the whole appearance and in the actual material of the other."[15]

Origen's analogy is helpful. It illustrates the Trinity's humility as the Father lovingly sends the Son to us in Jesus. Jesus is God come to us in a size we can receive and not be overwhelmed. He has literal human limbs. He has a human body that can be touched, for it is made out of matter. He is a walking illustration of the humility of God.

MESSIAH AND SON OF GOD

Erasmo Leiva-Merikakis draws our attention to "the factual truth of Jesus' innermost identity," his person as both a human being and as God. People had difficulty understanding this, whether they were friends or enemies of Jesus. "Peter, no more than Caiaphas or Satan himself, could not comprehend, much less accept, the compatibility and mysterious kinship intimately binding Jesus' divine identity as Son of God to his Passion and death."[16]

Caiaphas's question at Jesus' trial -- "Are you the Messiah, the Son of God?" – illustrates "the whole spiritual landscape of the Gospel."[17] For this is the question many asked of Jesus from the beginning of his ministry, and concerns what "Son of God" means. Let's explore this for a moment, with Leiva-Merikakis's guidance.

When Jesus is born, he is described as "Emmanuel," *God-with-Us*. At his baptism by John the Baptist and at his Transfiguration, the divine voice of the Father declares in identical words, this is *my beloved Son,* with whom I am well-pleased" (*Mt* 3:17, 17:5).

Not only does the voice of the Father declare Jesus to be his Son, but darker voices proclaim the same thing. Consider the voices of the

---

15. Origen, *On First Principles* 1.2.8; ACD 2.103.
16. Erasmo Leiva-Merikakis, *Heart of the Word: Meditations on the Gospel According to Saint Matthew*, Volume IV (San Francisco: Ignatius Press, 2021), 326.
17. Ibid., 327.

Gadarene demoniacs. "What have you to do with us, O Son of God? Have your come here to torment us before the time" (*Mt* 8:29)?

Merikakis, immersed in the thoughts of the church fathers, comments:

> Jesus' dynamic presence and deepest identity is a sort of radioactive power galvanizing all spirits, whether to declarations of salvation and love and to acts of pleading and adoration or to anguished, cowering, and spiteful rejection. The resplendent presence of Jesus of Nazareth at the Jordan and on Tabor even opens the heavens and calls forth the Father's testimony. Thus we clearly see that both the gloomy valleys of the denial of Jesus' identity as Son of God and the sun-drenched peaks of its proclamation, together, determine the spiritual geography of the Gospel. According to Matthew, the search for salvation and its finding are quite evidently tantamount to the quest for Jesus' divine sonship, followed by either embracing or rejecting it. In either case, a transcendental, life-changing event occurs.[18]

The devil and his demons reject Jesus for they knew who he was. Caiaphas and the Sanhedrin refuse to believe because they rejected the possibility that God could become a human being. For Jesus to proclaim his deity was to commit blasphemy, to lie about God. God could not become a human being, the Jewish leaders believed. Yet this was exactly what God had humbly done in the incarnation.

Athanasius teaches that Jesus's body was a real body, with all the characteristics of a human body. He reminds us that Thomas doubted that the resurrection had occurred, and that Jesus insisted that Thomas touch his body. "Thomas handled (*Jn* 20:26-27) and saw in it the marks of the nails that the Word himself endured . . ."[19]

Though the eternal Word was "incorporeal" and "intangible", the Son "appropriated to himself what belonged to the body as belonging to himself, the incorporeal Word." As we've seen earlier in this book, because the Word joined himself to human nature, we are able "to partake of the

---

18. Ibid.
19. Athanasius, *Letter to Epictetus* 6; ACD 2.106.

Godhead of the Word," God's intention for human nature from the beginning.[20]

PARTAKERS AND PARTICIPANTS IN THE DIVINE NATURE

Athanasius's amazing words are echoed by the church fathers as a whole. Before we consult them, though, let's return to Peter's words in 2 Peter 1:4. "Through these he has given us his very great and precious promises, so that through them you may participate in the divine nature, having escaped the corruption that is in the world caused by evil desires."

Now carefully read a variety of church fathers' comments on the implications of Peter's teaching in 2 Peter 1:4, our partaking or participating in the divine nature.

Origen sees us partaking through "the fellowship of the Holy Spirit." To be in fellowship with the Spirit is to participate in the divine nature.[21]

Novation, another ancient Christian writer, links participation to immortality. Human nature, now in Christ is "the companion of divinity, because divinity is immortal, and so immortality is the result of partaking in the divine nature."[22]

In a striking comment on the believer's bodily participation in Christ through the bread and wine of the Eucharist, Cyril of Jerusalem writes, "When Christ's body and blood become the tissue of our members, we become Christ-bearers and 'partakers of the divine nature,' as the blessed Peter said."[23]

This comment comes from Cyril's *Mystagogic Catechesis*, a series of talks he gave as bishop of Jerusalem to persons who had entered the church and could now receive the Eucharist. Cyril wants these new believers to recognize how close Christ now is to them. The "tissue" of their bodies has changed its nature and is now immortal, a point we just saw Novatian emphasizing.[24]

For Ambrose of Milan – the African Augustine's mentor – participa-

---

20. Ibid.
21. Origen, *Sermons on Leviticus* 4.4.2; ACCS New Testament, Volume XI, 132.
22. Novatian, *On the Trinity* 15.7; ACCS NT, Vol. XI, 132.
23. Cyril of Jerusalem, *Mystagogic Catechesis* 4, in The Early Church Fathers, *Cyril of Jerusalem*, Edward Yarnold, S.J., (London and New York: Routledge, 2000), 179.
24. Ibid.

tion in the divine nature points to the rational nature that all humans possess and "which makes us able to seek what is divine, which is not far from each one of us, in whom we live and are and move."[25]

Leo the Great encourages God's precious image-bearers to "Realize your dignity" as Christians, a good word especially when we feel attracted to sin. "Once you have been made a partaker of the divine nature, do not return to your former baseness by a life unworthy of that dignity. Remember whose head it is and whose body of which you constitute a member!"[26]

A favorite of mine is a comment by Hilary of Arles. Hilary captures the dynamic movement of grace shown to us in the incarnation and the amazing gift Christ offers us as we enter into union with him. "Just as God stepped out of his nature to become a partaker of our humanity, so we are called to step out of our nature to become partakers of his divinity."[27]

* * *

Pause and Reflect: Ponder Hilary's insight with me, a perception birthed directly from the second letter of the apostle Peter. The next time you are tempted to believe that God couldn't possibly love someone like you, return to Hilary's words. God's love for us in Christ and our participation in the divine nature is an effective antidote for spiritual discouragement and depression. Can you remember three times when you were spiritually discouraged? Write them down. How might Peter's words in his second letter have helped you to deal with your discouragement?

* * *

The Son of God has lovingly become a human being on our behalf. In doing so, Christ's dual nature -- his humanity and his deity -- enables atonement, but that is not all; the goal of salvation is our transformation

---

25. Ambrose, *Letters to Priests* 49; ACD 2.132.
26. Leo the Great, *Sermons* 21.3; ACD 2.133.
27. Hilary of Arles, *Introductory Commentary of 2 Peter*; ACD 2.133.

into Christ, the great image-bearer (*Col* 1:15ff). This was always God's design for human beings.

Now, Peter teaches, because of God's "great and precious promises" – all centered in and on Christ – we participate in the divine nature, not by ceasing to be human beings, but through our transformation into what God always desired for humans to be. God offers participation in his divine nature to us.

The Greek word in 2 Peter 1:4 for "sharers," "partakers," or "participants" is *koinōnoi*, the plural of the common Greek word *koinos*, often translated as "sharer," "associate," or "companion". For Africans, the idea of participation or solidarity with Christ resonates well with fundamental African values. Tegha A. Nji and Valery I. Akoh point to a number of African proverbs which teach "that participation is a core value of the African society":[28]

- One knee does not bring up a child (Sukuma).
- One hand does not nurse a child (Swahili).
- One finger does not kill a louse (a popular proverb that "appears in twenty-three East and Central African languages").
- One hand does not tie a bundle (Weh, Cameroon).
- When spider webs unite, they can tie up a lion (Amharic, Ethiopia).
- Unity is strength, division is weakness, and sharing is wealth (Swahili).
- It is easier to break a single broomstick but much more difficult to break a number of broomsticks.
- Teeth without gaps chew the meat (Ganda).
- Lack of unity spells weakness (Kikuyu).
- It takes a village to raise a child.
- Two hands wash each other (Akan, Zulu).
- Many beads form one necklace (Luo).
- When minds are one, what is far comes near (Swahili).
- It is a pain and curse to be alone (Akan).

---

28. "The African Understanding of Solidarity and the Ratzingerian Concept of Pro-Existence: A Mutually Beneficial Dialogue," Tegha A. Nji and Valery I. Akoh, 103, in *Joseph Ratzinger and the Future of African Theology*, edited by Maurice Ashley Agbaw and Matthew Levering (Eugene, Oregon: Wipf and Stock, 2021). The proverbs are found on 102-103.

- What is two are people, and what is one is animal (Akan).
- Two stones are not enough for cooking (Swahili).
- Not to aid one in distress is to kill him or her in your heart.
- The hen with chick does not swallow the worm (Sukuma).

Nji and Akoh then point to the insight of Joseph Ratzinger: "Christian faith is not based on the atomized individual but comes from the knowledge that there is no such thing as the mere individual, that on the contrary, man is himself only when he is fitted into the whole. . ."[29] "For Africans," Nji and Akoh observe, "the 'I' can only find its perfection when lived in the 'we' of the community, without at the same time losing its individuality."[30]

The heart of this African insight is Christological. In becoming human, the Son of God willingly and lovingly joins himself to us. He gives himself to us, body, mind, soul, and divinity. He desires to be one with us, and through intimate communion with humans to transform what we are into what he is.

In turn, as we are joined to Christ we become one with his body on earth, the church. The apostle Paul makes this clear in many places (1 *Cor* 12, 1 *Cor* 14); Christ's body the church consists of many different persons, each with their own particular gifting (1 *Cor* 12:4-11). Some are hands, some are eyes, some are feet (1 *Cor* 12:12-20). Yet they are all one in Christ, as Christ's church is one.

As we saw in our selection of African proverbs, the theme of oneness and solidarity is a commonplace in African cultures. "There is an African proverb which states that 'If you want to go fast, go alone; but if you want to go far, go with others.' By esteeming solidarity, Africans seek to go far. Given this background of solidarity, African Christians can understand what St. Cyprian means when he says, 'No one can have God for his Father, who does not have the Church for his mother.'"[31]

Surely this Christological and ecclesial concept of unity -- in the family, the community, and the church -- is related to the African under-

---

29. Ratzinger is quoted on p. 105 of Nji and Akoh; cf. Ratzinger, *Introduction to Christianity*, 245.
30. Nji and Akoh, op. cit., 109.
31. Ibid., 118; cf. Cyprian, *De Catholicae Ecclesiae Unitate* (On the Unity of the Catholic Church), 6.

standing of *ubuntu*. Nji and Akoh describe "a widely accepted definition of *ubuntu*" as

> popularized between 1993 by the following proverb of the Nguni Bantu people, in Southern Africa: '*umuntu ngumuntu ngabantu*,' translated as, 'a person is a person through other persons,' or 'I am because we are,' or 'I can only be a person through others.'[32]

Mercy Oduyoye writes of the African emphasis on

> life as life-in-community. We can only truly know ourselves if we remain true to our community, past and present. The concept of individual success or failure is secondary. The ethnic group, the village, the locality are crucial in one's estimation of oneself. Our nature as beings-in-relation is a two-way relation: with God and with our fellow human beings.[33]

How different from the Western view of the primacy of the individual!

Agbonkhianmeghe E. Orobator refers to the thought of Charles Nyamiti for the Christological implications of *ubuntu*. Nyamiti "maintains that we can talk of Jesus Christ as the elder brother 'of the multitude of God's children in whose veins – thanks to the mystery of the Incarnation – circulates the same life-blood of Jesus Christ.'" Orobator observes, "To say the church is a family of God means that it is modeled on the relationship that characterizes our Triune God as a communion of uniqueness, equality, and mutuality."[34]

THE IMPORTANCE OF 2 PETER 1:4

Let's return for a moment to the church fathers' interpretation of 2 Peter 1:4, where Peter writes that Christians are "partakers" or "participants" in

---

32. Nji and Akoh, "Joseph Ratzinger and the Future of African Theology," op. cit., 94.
33. Mercy Oduyoye, *The Value of African Beliefs and Theology for Christian Theology* (Maryknoll, N.Y.: Orbis Books, 1979), 110-111; quoted in Cedric Mayson, *Why Africa Matters* (Maryknoll, N.Y.: Orbis Books, 2010), 23.
34. Agbonkhianmeghe E. Orobator, *Theology Brewed in an African Pot* (Maryknoll, N.Y.: Orbis Books, 2009), 87.

the divine nature. Ponder more interpretive comments from the church fathers.

Bede, who fits in the category of both a patristic and medieval commentator, connects our knowledge of God and our realization of "the magnitude of his promises. When God blesses us, he changes our very being so that *whatever we were by nature is transformed* by the gift of His Holy Spirit, *so that we may truly become partakers of his nature.*"[35]

* * *

Pause and Reflect: Consider carefully Bede's words. God has promised to bless us. This blessing is the transformation of our "being." Human nature in Christ "is transformed by the gift of his Holy Spirit." The joyful result is that we "become partakers of his nature"; we are genuinely transformed through participation in the divine nature. As we are transformed by faith, Athanasius's words are fulfilled: "For he was incarnate so that we might be made God."[36] Is this a new idea for you? What do you think? Write down your response to Peter's and Athanasius's words.

* * *

Andreas, a monk who lived in the seventh century CE, collected commentary from previous church fathers and connected these insights into a linked interpretive chain, called a *catena*. In his comments on 2 Peter 1:4 we see these connections or links quite clearly. He writes:

> God has blessed us abundantly – that is the meaning of this passage. We have received thousands of good things as a result of Christ's coming, and through them we can become partakers of the divine nature and be turned toward life and godliness. Therefore we must behave in such a way as to

---

35. Bede, *On 2 Peter;* ACCS NT, Vol XI, 133; my emphasis.
36. St Athanasius the Great of Alexandria, *On the Incarnation,* Preface by C.S. Lewis, Translation and Introduction by John Behr (Yonkers, N.Y.: St. Vladimir's Seminary Press, 2011), 107.

add virtue to faith, and in virtue walk along the way which leads to godliness until we come to the perfection of all good things, which is love.[37]

Carefully consider the following summary of Andreas's teaching:

- We have been blessed "abundantly" by God in Christ.
- As a "result of Christ's coming," we have "received thousands of good things."
- Among these good things "we have become partakers of the divine nature."
- By participating in the divine nature, we are "turned toward life and holiness."
- Hence, "we must behave in such a way as to add virtue to faith, and in virtue walk along the way which leads to godliness. . ."
- As we walk in virtue, we will finally come "to the perfection of all good things, which is love."[38]

* * *

Pause and Reflect: Andreas reminds us, much like the African fathers, that the goal of deification or *theosis* is love. For the church fathers, *doctrine and practice are indissolubly wedded*. The goal of our study is not more knowledge. The goal is love, which is coupled to knowledge. If our knowledge doesn't lead to love, something has gone terribly wrong.

* * *

A WONDERFULLY SURPRISING STORY

The Christian story of salvation celebrated by the African church fathers is really quite beautiful, surprising, and unique in the ancient world. Ponder for a moment the phrase that has served for our reflections from the Nicene Creed. **"For us and for our salvation he came down from**

---

37. Andreas, *Catena*; ACCS NT Vol. XI, *James, 1-2 Peter, 1-3 John, Jude*, edited by Gerald Bray (Downers Grove: InterVarsity Press, 2000), 133.
38. Ibid.

heaven." This line of the Nicene Creed, though familiar to most Christians, was a significant surprise for Greeks who entered the Christian faith. As John McGuckin helpfully comments, "for the Hellenistic religious mentality ... deity must not be sullied by material chaos."[39]

Greeks kids, the vast majority boys, were raised in a philosophical and religious environment where salvation *entailed leaving this material world behind* as the human soul made its way back to God. The world, human bodies, and matter in general were considered hindrances to one's spiritual life. Plato coined a phrase – *soma sema* – "the body is a prison", to illustrate his belief that the body was a prison from which the soul must escape. Ancient Christians understood that the soul was indeed important – more important than the body it animates – but the body still mattered, and how we conducted ourselves in it.

For many Greeks the "fall" was the descent of souls into bodies. Hence, "salvation" involved the release of the soul from its embodiment, often through various spiritual disciplines. Knowledge of these spiritual truths, gained through philosophical reflection, would lead to freedom as the soul was released from the prison house of the body. Strands of ancient Christian thought wove themselves around this idea.

Do you perceive how this ancient perspective would struggle to embrace the heart of the Christian proclamation that Jesus' body – along with his soul – was raised from the dead? Many new Greek believers were surprised by the resurrection of Jesus' body. For they had been taught that God was interested in the soul, not the body. The body was viewed as a hindrance, rather than a help, to the spiritual life. Hence, to hear that "for us and for our salvation he came down from heaven," was quite a revolutionary statement.

Yet the Nicene Creed is insistent. God, in the person of the eternal Son, has entered human history, born as a baby boy to a young Jewish woman by the name of Mary, a member of the nation of Israel, a people who traced their beginning back to the earliest moments of creation in the book of Genesis. God, now incarnate in the person of Jesus Christ, came down from heaven to redeem and recreate his precious image-bearers and creation itself -- not to help people escape from it.

The law and the prophets consistently proclaim the goodness of

---

39. ACD 2.79.

creation, the fall as the result of temptation and sin, and center salvation around the specific expectation that God would finally save Israel – and through Israel the world – through a promised "anointed one," the Messiah. The great surprise for everyone was that the long-awaited Messiah – the anointed one of God – would actually be the incarnate Son of God, who "for us and our salvation came down from heaven."

So, there was important interpretive work for the church fathers to do. Greeks embracing the gospel would need help understanding that creation and the matter that composed it, were goods to be saved, not escaped. Genesis 1-2 celebrated the creation of the universe; the God of creation delighted in creating things – all kinds of things. God clearly liked "stuff." Jews, in turn, needed help in expanding their understanding of the person and work of the Messiah as they pondered the gospel message.

Both Gentile and Jewish Christians affirmed in the Nicene Creed that the preexistent Word (*logos*), the eternal Son, had entered the history of Israel and human history at large in the incarnate Son of God, Jesus Christ. He had come "from heaven" to restore, redeem, heal, and save.

It is now time to turn to the next clause of the Nicene Creed: ". . . **by the power of the Holy Spirit he became incarnate from the Virgin Mary, and was made man.**"

9
BY POWER

> **. . . by the power of the Holy Spirit he became incarnate from the Virgin Mary and was made man.**

In this chapter, we complete the sentence: "**by the power of the Holy Spirit he became incarnate from the Virgin Mary and was made man**." In this phrase we encounter two different persons for the first time: the Holy Spirit and the Virgin Mary. We also have our first specific mention of the incarnation. So, there are important persons, ideas, and actions we will cover in chapter nine, and we'll take our time.

"BY THE POWER OF THE HOLY SPIRIT. . ."

This is the first time the Nicene Creed mentions the Holy Spirit. If you have a copy of the creed in front of you, let your eye slip down toward the bottom. There you will find three important sentences concerning the Holy Spirit. It reads: "We believe in the Holy Spirit, the Lord, the giver of life, who proceeds from the Father and the Son. With the Father and the Son he is worshiped and glorified. He has spoken through the Prophets."

The line we are examining in this book regarding the Holy Spirit is short and succinct: "by the power of the Holy Spirit. . ." What can we initially learn from this line? We'll look for help in answering this question from significant African church fathers, and especially examine insights from Cyril of Alexandria, the archbishop of this important Egyptian city from 412 to 444 CE. Cyril is commenting on the Nicene Creed as stated in its final form in the creed of Constantinople in 381 CE.

This final form in known as "The Nicene-Constantinopolitan Creed," first formulated at Nicaea in 325 and further expanded at Constantinople in 381. What immediately catches our eye is an important expansion of what the creed says about the Holy Spirit. The Nicene Creed in 325 CE simply closed with the words, "We believe in the Holy Spirit." These words, while surely true, were not deemed sufficient by the church fathers; in the creed of 381 added words about the Holy Spirit appear.

* * *

Pause and reflect: As you consider the Holy Spirit, what questions arise in your mind? Try to list them on a piece of paper. Ancient Christians also had important questions about the Spirit. Is the Holy Spirit fully divine, like the Father and the Son? Or is the Holy Spirit an exalted creature? How is the Holy Spirit related to the Father and Son? Is the Spirit relationally distinct from them, a third person within the Holy Trinity? What difference does the answer we give to these questions have for our relationship with God?

* * *

The African bishop Athanasius, a key player in the formation of the Nicene Creed, strongly disagreed with those who believed the Holy Spirit to be a creature rather than God. He asked, "how can they dare to call the Spirit a created thing, when the Spirit has the same unity with the Son as the Son with the Father?"

The Holy Spirit is not a creature. If so, what conceptual problems may occur for us in understanding the nature and person of the Spirit? For example, some ancient Christians questioned whether the Holy Spirit shared the same divine essence with the Father and the Son. If the Spirit does not share the same essence, he must not be God. Athanasius comments: By "dividing the Spirit from the Word, they no longer safeguard the one Godhead in Trinity..."[1]

Athanasius understood that if the Holy Spirit is of a different essence or substance from that of the Father and Son, we end up with a picture of God as a very strange being, both "Creator and created."[2] That just won't do.

Cyril of Alexandria discerned the same problem Athanasius addressed. "... how can the Spirit be unequal in eternity to God the Father and the Son?"[3] How indeed? For if the Holy Spirit is not divine, the Trinity becomes a very strange communion of drastically unequal persons.

Do you see the problem? Cyril argues that the Holy Spirit possesses every attribute of God, including God's eternity. As eternal, the Holy Spirit has always existed, and shares God's essence with the Father and the Son.

Cyril writes: "When did he [the Holy Spirit] not exist, who is before all? For he is equal in substance to the Father and the Son?"[4] Since the Holy Spirit shares the divine essence with the Father and Son, the Holy Spirit is equally God with the Father and the Son. Does this mean that the Holy Spirit is not distinct relationally from the Father or the Son?

RELATIONAL DISTINCTIONS

Relational distinctions within the essence of God are a crucial characteristic of the Holy Trinity. The church formulated these distinctions on the basis of God's revelation in Jesus Christ, God incarnate. If Jesus was God and the Father was God, the church realized that a new model of God was necessary. Then, as the church pondered the Scripture, and its own practices in worship, the deity of the Holy Spirit became increasingly apparent. A triune model of God was the beautiful result of the church's deliberations.

Let's return to Cyril's thoughts. If the reality, wonder, and beauty of the Holy Trinity is a revelation from God, Cyril asked how one can best describe the relational distinctions between the persons of the Father,

---

1. Athanasius, *Letter to Serapion* 1.2; ACD 2.117.
2. Ibid.
3. Cyril of Alexandria, *Homilies on the Gospel of Luke* 38; ACD 2.120.
4. Ibid.

Son, and Holy Spirit, who shared the same essence. In answering this question, Cyril affirmed the Nicene Creed's statements and focuses his discussion on the relations between the persons.

Cyril describes the difference between the persons as relational, not essential. So, though the Holy Spirit is fully God, the Spirit is not the Father or the Son. Cyril puts it this way: "The Holy Spirit proceeds from God the Father as from the fountain, but the Spirit is not foreign to the Son. Every property of the Father belongs to the Word, who by nature was truly begotten from him."[5]

Cyril is using words very carefully. Did you notice that he said the Holy Spirit "proceeds" from the Father? Cyril uses a different word regarding the relation between the Father and the Son, describing the Son "by nature" as "truly begotten from him".

Now take a look at the Nicene Creed. When it describes Jesus Christ, it states he is "eternally begotten of the Father." Jesus is "begotten, not made." The Holy Spirit, however, is not begotten from the Father. Rather, the creed states that the Holy Spirit "proceeds" from the Father and the Son.

Cyril, then, realizes words such as "begotten" and "proceeds" are distinct relational terms used to distinguish the persons. They do not refer to the essence of God, but to the relations between the persons. The persons of the Trinity are distinct relationally, but not essentially. As Cyril writes,

> For the Holy Spirit indeed proceeds from God the Father but also belongs to the Son. It is even called the Spirit of Christ, though proceeding from God the Father . . . The Holy Spirit, therefore, indeed proceeds, as I have said, from God the Father, but his only-begotten Word, as being both by nature and truly Son, and resplendent with the Father's dignities, ministers the Spirit to the creation and bestows the Spirit on those who are worthy.[6]

* * *

Pause and Reflect: Are you feeling a bit overwhelmed by these

---
5. Ibid.
6. Ibid.

Trinitarian intricacies? Don't be discouraged. Catch your breath. The God you are learning about as the Holy Trinity is the God who invited you into relationship the first time you came to know him. He has not changed. It is your understanding of God that is expanding. Invite this deeper awareness to descend from your mind into your heart. Allow it to grow there like a seed. Water it with prayer, study, and meditation. As you ponder, note down any insights or questions that arise.

* * *

THE ASCENSION AND THE DESCENT OF THE HOLY SPIRIT

Let's continue to explore the relationship between the incarnation of the Son of God and the person and work of the Holy Spirit. We will do so from the perspective of Cyril, one of the great African theologians. I hope you get to know him well.

First, though, let's consider some important biblical texts related to our topic. We begin by turning to Acts 1. So much has taken place in the relationship between Jesus and the apostles. The disciples have learned that Jesus Christ, their teacher over the last three years, is actually God incarnate. They have witnessed Jesus' resurrection. And they have been instructed by Jesus to wait in Jerusalem for empowerment by the Holy Spirit. "I am going to send you what my Father has promised; but stay in the city until you have been clothed with power from on high" (*Lk* 24:49).

In Acts 1, Luke continues the narrative that he began in the gospel of Luke. Jesus has taught the disciples for forty days. With the end of this teaching, the time has now arrived for Jesus to ascend to heaven, and for the Holy Spirit to descend, for the Spirit will empower the disciples for the mission Jesus has given them: "You will receive power when the Holy Spirit comes on you; and you will be my witnesses in Jerusalem, and in all Judea and Samaria, and to the ends of the earth. After he had said this, he was taken up before their very eyes, and a cloud hid him from their sight" (*Acts* 1:9).

In Cyril's commentary on John's gospel, he teaches that God set "the coming of Christ as the time for the Holy Spirit to descend on us. He promises this; 'In those days I will pour out my Spirit manifestly and clearly on all flesh' (*Joel* 2:28)."[7] Cyril describes the descent of the Spirit as a sign of God's "generosity and liberality," the time when "the Only-Begotten" came to "the earth in flesh, as a man born of woman according to the holy Scripture." God the Father, who is the source of the Son, also "gave the Holy Spirit." It is Christ "who received the Spirit first, as the firstfruits of the renewed nature."[8]

Did Christ receive something he didn't already have? "In no way!," Cyril writes. "The Spirit belongs to the Son. He is not sent into him from outside, as God bestows the Spirit in us. The Spirit is naturally in him just as he is in the Father. The Spirit proceeds through him to the saints as the Father bestows him on each one in the appropriate way. We say that the Son received the Spirit insofar as he had become human, and it was appropriate for him to receive him as a human."[9]

The Son is fully God, as is the Father and the Spirit. As such, the Son has never been apart from or bereft of the Holy Spirit. In the incarnation, though, the human nature of the incarnate Jesus receives the Holy Spirit, the firstfruits of the renewal of human nature itself. "As human, he had the whole of human nature in himself, in order to renew all of humanity and restore it to its original state . . . ."[10]

* * *

Pause and Reflect: Ponder for a moment the wonder of who you are as a human being and what God has done on your behalf. Your human nature was corrupt and dying. The only future awaiting you was death and the corruption of the grave. Not only has God said a loud "No" to this bleak expectation; he has acted to reverse what has happened. All things – including your human nature – are being renewed and recreated in Christ.

* * *

---

7. Cyril of Alexandria, *Commentary on the Gospel of John* 5.2; ACD 2.117.
8. Ibid., ACD 2.117-118.
9. Ibid., ACD 2.118.
10. Ibid.

Try listing your attitudes and behaviors before coming into relationship with Christ. Take your time. Now, draw a line through all you've listed. For in union with Jesus, your human nature is being healed through the Holy Spirit. The human race in Christ has received a new beginning, and that includes you!

This is what Cyril means by the "second commencement of our race . . ."[11] Cyril writes,

> As human, he had the whole of human nature in himself, in order to renew all of humanity . . . The Only-Begotten became human like us so that the good things that were returned and the grace of the Spirit might first be grounded in him and thereby firmly preserved for the whole nature.[12]

This exalted reality – the restoration of human nature as it was always meant to be – is established and firm. Indeed, Cyril teaches, the "stability that is proper to his nature" has in Christ been "extended" to us, "to the human nature that in Adam had been condemned to be changeable and prone to both error and perversion."[13]

Yes, "the fall of the first human resulted in a loss for all humanity." That is not the end of the story, though, for "the whole race has acquired the benefit of the divine gifts in him who knows no change."[14] Be encouraged. God is not going to change his mind and purposes for you as his precious image-bearer. You are moving progressively into what God had always meant you to be, and that is a very good thing!

Cyril delights in the mystery of Christ's person as both human and divine. In his human nature, Jesus endures the weaknesses we all experience, finally dying on the cross for us, emptying himself in self-sacrificial love on our behalf (cf. *Phil* 2:5-11). Still, the "fullness" of his divine nature remains, even as he suffers in his human nature. Indeed, Cyril teaches, because Jesus is God, fully divine with the Father and the Holy Spirit, he possesses the power to send the Holy Spirit after his ascension into heaven.

Cyril considers the power to send the Holy Spirit "of great importance

---

11. Cyril of Alexandria, *Homilies on the Gospel of Luke* 11; ACD 2.119.
12. Cyril of Alexandria, *Commentary on the Gospel of John* 5.2; ACD 2.118.
13. Ibid.
14. Ibid.

for the proof and demonstration that Jesus is God and Lord."[15] Because the incarnate Christ shares in God's "Substance," he "can bestow on humans the indwelling of the Holy Spirit." The result, Cyril believes, is that human beings become "partakers of the divine nature" in Christ (cf. 2 Pet 1:4). All these wonders are possible because of Christ's person as both fully human and fully divine, in constant relationship with the Father and the Holy Spirit.[16]

Don't think, though, that the descent of the Holy Spirit to us – the Son's gift to us -- indicates that the Holy Spirit is in any way inferior to the Son. In his third letter to Nestorius, Cyril writes that the Spirit is to be distinguished from the Son, "yet he is not therefore alien from the Son. For he is indeed called the Spirit of Truth, and Christ is the Truth, and he is poured forth from him just as he is also from God the Father."[17] Again, we see that Father, Son, and Holy Spirit share a common essence, but are relationally distinct.

The thoughts of the great African bishop Athanasius are also helpful. Athanasius teaches that before the Son's incarnation, the Son of God existed as God the eternal Word, God's *logos* (cf. Jn 1:1). Athanasius points to the divine *logos* as the one who supplies the Spirit to "the saints."[18]

As the incarnate Word, Jesus continues to supply the Spirit. For instance, toward the close of his earthly ministry, Jesus breathes on the apostles and says, "Receive the Holy Spirit" (Jn 20:22). He had the right and power to breathe out the Spirit as the divine Word. And we, as human beings, "have in him and through him the source of our receiving these things."[19]

The connection between Jesus and his followers, Athanasius teaches, is extremely intimate. "For when he is said to be anointed as man, it is we who are anointed in him. When he is baptized, it is we who are baptized in him."[20]

---

15. Cyril of Alexandria, *Homilies on the Gospel of Luke* 10; ACD 2.119.
16. Ibid.
17. Cyril of Alexandria, *Third Letter to Nestorius* (Letter 17); ACD 2.118.
18. Athanasius, *Against the Arians* 1.48; ACD 2.117.
19. Ibid.
20. Ibid.

A BRIEF WORD FROM BASIL THE GREAT ON THE HOLY SPIRIT

Let's take a brief look at a treatise titled *On the Holy Spirit*, by of one of the great Cappadocian church fathers, Basil the Great. Among other things, Basil argues that the Holy Spirit couldn't do the kinds of things the Spirit does unless the Holy Spirit is God. For instance, Basil points to the giving of resurrection life as an act that only God can do. Basil writes: "Resurrection from the dead is accomplished by the operation of the Spirit . . . He gives us risen life, refashioning our souls in the spiritual life."[21]

Basil concludes it's impossible for the church to give the Holy Spirit too much honor, as some Christians who opposed the deity of the Holy Spirit were reluctant to do. How can the Christian "be afraid of giving the Spirit too much honor? We should instead fear that even though we ascribe to Him the highest titles we can devise, or our tongues can pronounce, our Ideas about Him might still fall short."[22]

Hence, when the Nicene Creed states that "by the power of the Holy Spirit he became incarnate from the Virgin Mary and was made man," always remember that the Holy Spirit can do such wondrous deeds because the Holy Spirit is God, as is the Father and the Son.

---

21. Basil the Great, *On the Holy Spirit*, trans. David Anderson (Crestwood, N.Y.: St. Vladimir's Press, 1980), 77-78.
22. Ibid.

10

INCARNATION

...he became incarnate...

The African church fathers strongly affirmed the Nicene Creed's statement that the Son of God "became incarnate." They believed, along with the rest of the church, that Jesus Christ was fully human and fully divine, and had been born in our world as Jesus of Nazareth. They believed this because of the biblical testimony regarding Jesus.

As ancient Christians declared their belief in the incarnation, they never tried to explain how Jesus could be both human and divine. For such was a mystery beyond the church's comprehension. They knew the incarnation to be true. How it could be true was a different matter. The church fathers saw the incarnation as a mystery to be adored in worship, not explained according to logical categories.

Indeed, the incarnation is a mystery, for how is it possible for a human being to be God, or for God to become a human being, a human male born to the Virgin Mary? How could both of these statements be simultaneously true?

The church never comprehended how Jesus Christ could be fully God and fully human. Rather, the church fathers gathered at Nicaea in 325 produced clear and profound statements in the Nicene Creed that *protected and preserved* the mystery of the incarnation. Jesus was not partly human and partly God. No, he was fully human and fully God from the moment of his conception in Mary's womb by the power of the Holy Spirit.

Fully God? Absolutely. The Nicene Creed proclaims that every attribute we predicate of God to be true of Jesus: omnipotence, omnipresence, omniscience, and so on. Jesus as God possesses infinite power, is fully present everywhere in the universe, and knows everything it is possible to know. All the characteristics of God we find in the Bible are absolutely true of Jesus. If God is infinitely righteous, so is Jesus. If God is infinite love, so is Jesus (cf. 1 *Jn* 4:16). Jesus is fully God. The incarnation changed none of this, for *God cannot stop being God.*

And yet the incarnation proclaims that Jesus is also fully human, with all the characteristics of a human male, apart from sin. How can a single person can be both divine and human? We don't know. Our ability to comprehend the mystery of the incarnation breaks down. One reality would seem to rule out the other. Yet, as we'll see the African church fathers teaching without reservation, humanity and deity were both absolutely true of Jesus, and still are to this very day.

Sometimes when we feel confused or daunted by the mystery of the incarnation, we may be tempted to resolve the inherent tension it presents by modifying either of its poles. "Jesus was fully human, but not fully God." "Jesus was fully God, but not fully human."

In the church's history, the wisest theologians – almost all of whom were pastors, bishops, and leaders – learned to think reverently and wisely about the incarnation. With equal emphasis, *they affirmed Christ's deity and humanity* and worshiped Jesus as the savior of Israel and the world. The worst theologians attempted to reduce the inherent tension the mystery of the incarnation presents, and denied either Christ's deity or his humanity.

THE SURPRISING ROLE OF HERESY

Let's pause for a moment to consider the question of heresy. This is not a popular word in Western culture and is viewed with suspicion by many. In the history of the ancient church, though, heresy performed a positive role, for the views of "heretics" often spurred the church to seek the truth with greater clarity. Faulty teaching prodded the church to understand the person of Christ more clearly, both in terms of his deity and humanity.

Exactly what is a heresy? The African Tertullian, writing in the early third century CE, argued that heresy could be identified by its divergence from apostolic teaching and doctrine. He describes a distinct and identifiable pattern of revelation and authority. First, Tertullian teaches, Jesus in his earthly ministry

> declared what he was, what he had been, what was the Father's will which he was carrying out, what was the conduct he laid down for humankind: all this he declared either openly to the people or privately to the disciples.[1]

Tertullian explains that Jesus chose twelve leaders to be his "close companions," men who proceeded to plant churches throughout the Mediterranean basin. As they did so they "published the same doctrine of the same faith."[2] These apostolically founded churches, planted by the very men who had been chosen by Jesus to be the authoritative interpreters of the meaning of his life and work, were all part of one connected plant or vine.

Tertullian teaches that newer churches "borrowed the shoot of faith and the seeds of doctrine" from those churches previously planted. It is this shared seed, a dissemination of apostolic life and doctrine, that identifies a church as

> apostolic, as being the offspring of apostolic churches. Every kind of thing must needs be classed with its origin. And so the churches, many and great as they are, are identical with that one primitive Church issuing from the Apostles, for thence they are all derived. So all are primitive and all apostolic, while all are one.[3]

---

1. Tertullian, *Prescription Against Heretics* 20, cited in Henry Bettenson, ed. and trans., *The Early Christian Fathers: A Selection from the Writings of the Fathers from St. Clement of Rome to St. Athanasius* (London: Oxford University Press, 1956), 190. I have slightly modified the bumpy translation.
2. Ibid.
3. Ibid.

Only preaching and doctrine that matches apostolic teaching, Tertullian writes, should be received in the church. Carefully ponder his words:

Now the substance of their preaching, that is, Christ's revelation to them, must be approved, on my ruling, only through the testimony of those churches which the Apostles founded by preaching to them both with a living voice and afterwards by their letters. If this is so, it is likewise clear that all doctrine which accords with these apostolic churches, the sources and origins of the faith, must be reckoned as truth, since it maintains without doubt what the churches received from the Apostles, the Apostles from Christ, and Christ from God . . . We are in communion with the apostolic churches because there is no difference of doctrine. This is our guarantee of truth.[4]

What, then, is heresy? For the African Tertullian at least, heresy is instruction that can by identified by proposing doctrine at variance with the teaching of the apostles. As Tertullian writes, heresy "originates neither from an apostle nor from an apostolic man; for the Apostles would not have diverged from one another in doctrine; no more would the apostolic man have put out teaching at variance with that of the apostles."[5]

Remember the question we are exploring in this chapter. Exactly who is Jesus Christ? When we ask this question, we immediately face two further questions the Nicene Creed addresses. Is Jesus Christ God? Is Jesus Christ human? What does the Nicene Creed mean when it affirms the incarnation of the Son of God?

THE DEITY OF JESUS CHRIST

Is Jesus Christ God? If so, how are we to understand his deity? Ancient Christians proposed various answers to this question. Let's take a look at them, sifting through them with our ancient brothers and sisters. This winnowing process took a number of years. Consider some of the proposals made by ancient Christians:

---

4. Ibid, 191.
5. Ibid, 191.

- Maybe there were three gods: the Father, the Son, and the Holy Spirit.

- Perhaps Jesus was a lesser god, much as there were greater or lesser gods in the Greek and Roman pantheon. He was in some sense divine, but not fully divine as the Father.

- Conceivably there was only one God, but that single God possessed the marvelous ability to manifest himself in various forms or roles, occasionally as Father and at other times in human history as the Son or the Holy Spirit.

These are only a sample of some of the proposals people made to answer the questions Jesus' deity raised. The church was attempting to answer the following questions:

- Was Jesus fully divine like God the Father, possessing all the attributes of God?

- If Jesus did possess all of God's attributes, what distinguished God the Son from God the Father?

- Was the difference between God the Father and God the Son real? Or was the difference simply a role that God manifested himself in history, sometimes as the Father, sometimes as the Son, and sometimes as the Holy Spirit?

Let's consider the proposal offered by Sabellius. Sabellius was an ancient Christian who taught that God manifested himself differently as God's plan for human history progressed. First, God presented himself as the Father up to the time of Jesus. Then God presented himself as Jesus Christ, as God's redemptive plan was further revealed to Israel and the surrounding nations. Finally, God assumed the role of the Holy Spirit.

Note that Sabellius believed the relational distinctions between Father, Son, and the Holy Spirit were not eternal. God was not eternally Father. God was not eternally Son. God was not eternally Holy Spirit. Why? If these distinctions were eternal, Sabellius reasoned we would necessarily have three Gods, not one. And he knew the Bible taught there was only one God. God was one, not three. Hence, there couldn't be eternal relational distinctions within the being or essence of God. Rather, the "Father" was like a mask God wore at one time; the mask of the Father was a mode through which God manifested himself; then as history progressed God wore the mask of the Son, and finally God wore the mask of the Spirit.

This solution appealed to some, for it seemed to solve the logical tensions produced by a robust, eternal relational distinction between the persons of the Trinity. Sabellius seemed to have resolved the problem posed by the Trinitarian arithmetic. God was one, but not three.

Do you perceive the error in Sabellius's proposal? The apostle John clearly distinguishes Jesus from the Father (cf. *Jn* 16:28, *Jn* 14:15-27). Other texts in John's gospel speak of the Father sending the Holy Spirit (*Jn* 14:26). Sabellius's attempt to foreclose the possibility of eternal relational distinctions between the Father, Son, and Spirit was a grave error. His proposal failed to satisfy the clear teaching of Scripture.

A more serious threat to the deity of Jesus Christ is found in the ideas of Arius.[6] Arius argued that the Son did not share the Father's substance or essence (Gk. *ousia*). Rather, the Son was an exalted creature, elevated above all others, but still a creation of God. Arius writes that "God was not always a Father," "The Son was not always," "the Word of God himself was 'made out of nothing,'" "Once He was not," "He was not before His origination," and "He as others 'had an origin of creation.'"[7]

Arius's insistence that the Son was an elevated creature birthed the rich Christological theology of the fourth century and, towards its conclusion, a much-needed exploration of the person and work of the Holy Spirit.

Once again, we see the surprisingly positive role heresy plays when the church discerns its presence. Heresy spurred the church to think and express itself more clearly. If Arius had not questioned Christ's deity, the church would have been less motivated to explore and express the wonder of Christ as God incarnate. Arius's ideas forced it to do so.

---

6. Here I will be drawing on ideas adapted from Roger E. Olson & Christopher A. Hall, *The Trinity* (Grand Rapids: Eerdmans, 2002), 32-49.
7. Arius as quoted by Athanasius in his *Four Discourses Against the Arians*, NPNF Second Series, Volume 4 (Peabody, Mass.: Hendrickson, 1994), 308-309.

Arius believed that many biblical texts supported his ideas. For instance, in the garden of Gethsemane Jesus experienced grief and fear. Arius couldn't reconcile these emotions with his understanding of God.

And what of the questions Jesus asked during his lifetime? If he were God, he would know all things. Yet Jesus asks questions that indicate his knowledge was incomplete. For instance, he asks the disciples how many loaves of bread they have at the feeding of the five thousand (*Mk* 6:38). Jesus teaches that the Son does not know when all things would "be accomplished" (cf. *Mk* 13:4, 32). These questions, Arius argued, indicated the Father's knowledge is clearly greater than that of the Son. If so, the Son could not be God. For shared deity necessitated shared attributes. If the Son was ignorant of the timing of the consummation of the age, he could not be God. Or, at least, Arius so believed.

KEY PLAYERS IN THE FORMATION OF THE NICENE CREED: ATHANASIUS AND GREGORY OF NAZIANZUS

As we've seen, in his response to Arian ideas, Athanasius analyzed the relationship between Jesus' humanity and his deity. He does so at length in *Four Discourses Against the Arians*. Athanasius contended that the "scope and character of Scripture presented a double account of the Savior."[8] The four gospels affirmed *both* the deity and humanity of Christ. Arian interpretations failed to recognize that some biblical texts referred to teaching, events, and actions of Christ related to his humanity, while others focused on Jesus' deity, as he taught and acted as *God* incarnate.

As the incarnate *Son*, Christ exists as the "Father's Word and Radiance and Wisdom." In the incarnation, the Son humbly assumes human flesh derived from "a Virgin, Mary, Bearer of God, and was made man."[9] The Word (*logos*) is "not external" to the human nature the Son assumes. Rather, Athanasius teaches, the incarnate Son lives and ministers in incomprehensible union with *both* his deity and humanity.

When Jesus healed the mother-in-law of Simon Peter, "He stretched forth His hand humanly, but He stopped the illness divinely."[10] When he

---

8. Athanasius, *Four Discourses Against the Arians*, op. cit., 411.
9. Ibid.
10. Ibid.

healed the man born blind from birth, "human was the spittle which He gave forth from the flesh, but divinely did He open the eyes through the clay."[11] At the raising of Lazarus, Jesus "gave forth a human voice, as man; but divinely, as God, did He raise Lazarus from the dead."[12]

Athanasius views the Son's incarnate actions as manifesting the intimate union in his person between his humanity and his deity. When Jesus grieved or expressed other human emotions, this was appropriate, for he was genuinely human, and Scripture contained texts expressing this reality. For "it was proper for the Lord, in putting on human flesh, to put it on whole with the affections proper to it..."[13]

The Nicene Creed, with the aid of leaders such as Athanasius, affirms both the humanity of Christ and his eternal generation by the Father. The eternal Son is divine, *homoousios* or of the "same essence" or "being" as the Father, while the incarnate Jesus is both human and divine.

Gregory of Nazianzus, an Eastern church father from Cappadocia, was acquainted with Athanasius's theology. He made important contributions of his own in refuting Arian ideas.

Gregory preached a series of sermons attacking Arianism in the latter stages of the fourth century. In these "orations" Gregory focused his attention on Eunomius and his followers. These were a radical Arian group who prided themselves on their supposed ability to plumb the mystery of the Trinity and to solve its inherent theological tensions through the formulation of rational syllogisms.

In his orations, Gregory eviscerates the Eunomian position. Elsewhere I have written that the Eunomians believed that

> anyone with an ounce of sense ... would surely recognize that there was only one God, the Father. To predicate further personal distinctions within God's being was to speak incomprehensible gibberish. In fact, there was scant room in Eunomian thought for incomprehensibility or mystery of any sort.[14]

---

11. Ibid.
12. Ibid.
13. Ibid.
14. Christopher A. Hall, *Reading Scripture with the Church Fathers* (Downers Grove: InterVarsity Press, 1998), 69.

In his orations, Gregory defends the deity of the Son and the Holy Spirit by proposing the idea of progressive revelation. Carefully consider Gregory's words: "The Old Testament proclaimed the Father openly, and the Son more obscurely. The New manifested the Son, and suggested the deity of the Spirit dwells among us, and supplies us with a clearer demonstration of himself."[15]

As God's plan and purposes in human history expand, so does his revelation. Why did God choose to reveal himself in such a slow, revelatory progression? Human beings at the biblical story's beginning simply weren't ready to grasp the end. ". . . [I]t was not safe, when the Godhead of the Father was not yet acknowledged, plainly to proclaim the Son; nor when that of the Son was not received, to burden us further (if I may use so bold an expression) with the Holy Ghost."[16]

God apparently likes to begin where people are, and then moves them to a new place in their understanding and relationship with him. God is not in a rush to accomplish his purposes. He takes his time.

Pause and reflect: Can you think of times, places, or circumstances where you rushed, when the Lord was saying, "Slow Down!" God is not in a hurry. God moves slowly in our lives and, I think, would encourage us to learn and grow at his pace, not our own. Sometimes we believe we're walking faithfully with Jesus and he's calling, "I'm back here!" Thinking well theologically is not to be rushed. Some truths – I'm thinking of the Holy Trinity – take a long time to grow well in our understanding and our lives. Where might the Lord be asking you to slow down? In your study? In your prayer life? What other areas might come to mind? List two or three.

Though we rightly distinguish between the persons of the Trinity, always

---

15. Gregory of Nazianzus, "The Fifth Theological Oration – on the Spirit," in *Christology of the Later Fathers*, ed. Edward R. Hardy (Philadelphia: Westminster Press, 1954), 207.
16. Ibid.

remember that these distinctions are relational in nature, with the three persons sharing fully the same divine essence. We worship only one God, not three. The African fathers were of one mind with the Cappadocian fathers (Gregory of Nazianzus, Basil the Great, Gregory of Nyssa) on this very point.

Phillip Cary reminds us that the Cappadocians believed that "all general terms (wisdom, power, goodness) refer to God in the singular; there is only one wisdom, one power, one goodness in God, not three."[17] Not only so, but the will and activity of God are one. Hence, all the analogies we draw from human life to illustrate the relationship between the persons ultimately break down. For instance, Jane and John might share a common human nature, but could choose as individual persons to exercise their wills in opposition to one another. "I want you to go shopping," Jane says to John. "No, I want to watch the Eagles game." Here two wills are clearly in conflict with one another. This never, ever happens with the persons of the Trinity. If even the possibility of this happening were true, we'd be dealing with three gods, not one.

Jane and John who are individual, separate persons can surely exercise their wills in opposition to each other. This doesn't happen with the persons of the Trinity because all three persons are *one in their will and activity*. They are not autonomous persons, like human beings, each with his own separate "ego" and "center" of consciousness. Rather, they have always and will always purpose and operate with one will and action. They are one God, not three. Cary helpfully comments: ". . . God is *not* three persons in the modern sense of the word – for three distinct divine persons, with three distinct minds, wills and centers of consciousness, would surely be three Gods (just as the Cappadocians said)."[18]

What about the gospel narratives? They clearly present Jesus as submitting his will to the will of the Father. If God's will is one, and the Son is one of the three persons in the Trinity, why would Jesus the Son submit his will to the Father? Their will is one, for God is one. Yes, this is true, the African fathers argued. But what of Jesus' human will? His human will, just like ours, must submit to the will of God.

---

17. Phillip Cary, "Historical Perspectives on Trinitarian Doctrine," *Religious and Theological Studies Fellowship Bulletin* (November-December 1995), 4.
18. Ibid., 5.

The distinction between the words *theologia* and *oikonomia* are helpful at this point. *Theologia* concerns God and Trinitarian relationships, while *oikonomia* or "economy" refers to God's purposes and actions in human history. An essential aspect of God's *oikonomia* concerns the incarnation of Jesus Christ. And what happened in the incarnation? God the Son became a human being, while never ceasing to be God.

We shouldn't be surprised, then, that some biblical texts refer to Christ's human nature expressing itself, such as Mark 14:6, where Jesus says in the garden of Gethsemane, "Yet not what I will, but what you will." In the garden Jesus' human will is expressing its desire and willingness to submit to the will of the Father.

To repeat, Jesus Christ has a human will and a divine will. How can this be? You're staring square in the face the mystery of the incarnation, and the mystery of the Holy Trinity. The Nicene Creed never attempts to explain these inherent mysteries; it simply wants to faithfully express, preserve and protect them.

AUGUSTINE'S THOUGHT ON THE TRINITY

It is impossible to treat in depth Augustine's thought on the Trinity in this short book. What we can provide is an outline of sorts, and encourage you to read Augustine himself.

Augustine writes that there "is the Father and the Son and the Holy Spirit – each one of these is God, and all of them together are one God; each of these is a full substance and all together are one substance."[19]

Augustine then distinguishes between the three persons, while rightly affirming that each person's attributes as God are identical. They "have the same eternal nature, the same unchangeableness, the same majesty, the same power." Augustine proceeds to locate the unity of the persons, not in the divine essence, but in the Father. "In the Father there is unity . . . . And the three are all one because of the Father . . ."[20]

Perhaps the best and simplest introduction to Augustine on the Trinity is found in a sermon he preached titled "Of the Words of St. Matthew's

---

19. Augustine, *On Christian Teaching* (Oxford: Oxford University Press, 1997), 10.
20. Ibid., 10.

Gospel, chap. 3:13: 'Then Jesus came from Galilee to the Jordan to John, to be baptized by Him.' Concerning the Trinity."[21]

In this sermon Augustine summarizes the thoughts found in his much longer work *On the Trinity*. The sermon is an excellent place to begin to understand Augustine on the Trinity. He addresses a number of important questions:

1. Does the Father ever act separately from the Son? Or the Son from the Father? Augustine's answer is no. From the inseparable nature of the work of the Father and the Son comes a second question.

2. If the Father does nothing apart from the Son and vice versa, was the Father "born of the Virgin Mary"? Did he suffer under Pontius Pilate? Did the Father rise again from the dead and ascend to heaven? Augustine responds no. He was well aware of the danger of patripassionism.

Patripassianism is a form of modalism or Sabellianism. "Patripassianism" literally means "the suffering of the Father." Recall that Sabellius argued that the relational distinctions between the persons were actually modes of God's revelation, masks that God wore as history progressed.

For the modalist, God was one; it was impossible for God to be three. Hence, some in the Western church argued that it was the Father who had become incarnate in Christ and suffered on the cross, for there was only one God. The church rejected this idea as a serious error. The Father and the Son are distinct persons.

3. In what sense can we say that the work of the Father and Son is inseparable? That's a good question. How does Augustine respond? "The Son indeed and not the Father was born of the Virgin Mary; but this birth of the Son, and not of the Father, was the work of both the Father and the Son. The Father did

---

21. Augustine, *Sermons on Selected Lessons of the New Testament*, Sermon 2, NPNF First Series, Vol. 6 (Peabody, Mass: Hendrickson, 1994), 262. I have tried to smooth out the bumpy King James English.

not rise again, but the Son, yet the resurrection of the Son was the work of the Father and the Son."[22]

Augustine proceeds to teach that trustworthy trinitarian theology finds its source in a heart and mind trained in humility, and ready to receive what God has said about himself. The best theology blossoms in a person who humbly accepts and worships the mysterious depth of the Trinity. Augustine urges us to

> remember who we are, and of Whom we speak. Let this and that, or whatever appertains to the nature of God, be with a pious faith embraced, with a holy respect entertained... For it is not of such a nature as it can ascend into the heart of man; but the heart of man must itself ascend to it.[23]

Isn't it wondrous and wild that human beings like you and me can think and speak of God? How can we ever do so adequately? Safely? Wisely? Discerningly? The subject is too high. Too holy. Augustine knew this full well.

> For if you have been able to comprehend what you would say, it is not God; if you have been able to comprehend it, you have comprehended something else instead of God. If you have been able to comprehend Him as you think, by so thinking you have deceived yourself.[24]

Are we simply stuck, frozen in silence, mute when it comes to speech about God? Augustine coaches his listeners to search for an analogy on a more attainable, humble plane, a "resemblance" we might find among God's creation.

> You were speaking of the Trinity of Majesty ineffable, and because you did fail in contemplating the Divine Nature, and with becoming humility did confess your infirmity, you did come down to human nature; pursue your inquiry there.[25]

---

22. Ibid.
23. Ibid.
24. Ibid., 263.
25. Ibid.

Human nature? Why would we look for analogies of the Trinity there? Augustine reminds us that *we are creatures made in the image of God.* "For God made man after His own image and likeness. Search then in your own self, if perhaps the image of the Trinity might bear some resemblance to the Trinity. And what is this image?"[26]

Augustine directs us to the human mind, "the inner man." Are there clues in the human mind, imprints of the divine, that can help us to understand the Trinity of the Father, Son, and Holy Spirit more clearly? Augustine thinks so.

MEMORY, UNDERSTANDING, AND WILL

In his famous analogy, Augustine focuses on the memory, the understanding, and the will. The memory retains, but only through the operation of the understanding and the intent of the will to do so. "Memory," Augustine writes, "is the name of one only of those three, yet all the three concurred in producing the name of this single one of the three. The single word 'memory' could not be expressed, but by the operation of the will, and the understanding, and the memory." In turn, "the single word 'understanding' could not be expressed, but by the operation of the memory and the understanding and the will."[27]

Augustine refrains from trying to identify the memory, understanding, or will with a specific person of the Trinity, counseling us to "leave somewhat to meditation and to silence." Instead, he encourages us to "believe that the Father, and the Son, and Holy Spirit may be exhibited separately, by certain visible symbols, by certain forms borrowed from the creatures, and still their operations be inseparable."[28]

Memory, will, and understanding appear to operate well as an analogy for the persons of the Trinity. Beware, though, of thinking that these analogies "are in any sort to be equaled with the Holy Trinity, to be squared after an analogy; that is, a kind of exact rule of comparison."[29] "We can know what is in us, but what is in Him who made you whatever it be, how can you know? And if you shall be ever able, you are not able

---

26. Ibid.
27. Ibid., 265.
28. Ibid.
29. Ibid.

yet. And even when you shall be able, will you be able to know God, as He knows himself?"[30] Of course, the answer is no.

The acuity and agility of this great African's mind, demonstrated as he grapples with trinitarian mysteries, has been acknowledged by his friends and foes, past and present. For Augustine, however, a holy life was more important than a finely tuned mind. He understood that spiritual insight and holiness of life were inextricably linked. Theology was to be practiced with the mind in the heart; a diseased life would lead to a diseased theology.

The church fathers believed the opposite was also true; a holy life filled with the presence of Christ would surely nurture the intellect's ability to reason well and humbly. Holy, loving character is necessary if holy things are to be understood and expressed well.

In speaking of the relationship between the Father and Son, Augustine comments that "seeing [that] this is a great mystery, *our conduct must be fashioned, that it may be comprehended.* For to the unworthy is it closed up; it is opened to those who are properly prepared for it." To seek after truth is for those whose life knocks on the door of the Lord. *"It is the life which knocks, it is to the life that it is opened.* The seeking is with the heart, the opening is to the heart."[31]

A DEEPER DIVE INTO THE WONDER OF JESUS CHRIST'S HUMANITY

If Jesus was divine, could he be genuinely human? A variety of responses were offered by the ancient church, some much better than others. Some argued that Jesus possessed a human body controlled by a divine mind. Others believed his body wasn't real. It only seemed to be a body. To what extent was Jesus human after all? Perhaps he was more like an angel. And how is Jesus' work as Lord and Savior related to who he is? What must he be for his work to be accomplished?

* * *

---

30. Ibid., 266.
31. Augustine, *Sermons*, Sermon 41, NPNF First Series (Peabody, Mass: Hendrickson, 1994), 398. My italics: I have occasionally smoothed out the stilted translation; the italics are mine.

Pause and reflect: Before reading further, pause and write out your understanding of Jesus' humanity as you presently grasp it. Then continue reading. How did you do when comparing your thoughts with African church fathers such as Augustine or Cyril of Alexandria. What did they teach you that you didn't know?

* * *

Cyril of Alexandria responded to the questions we have posed with a clear answer; Christ's person and Christ's work are intimately related. In a word, because Jesus was *both* human and divine, he could accomplish the work his Father asked him to do. Augustine also saw this clearly. If Jesus wasn't fully divine, he couldn't save us from the contamination of our sin, for only God can save. And if Jesus wasn't fully human, he couldn't redeem us from the ravages of sin, for every characteristic of who are as humans needs to be saved, rescued, and healed: our body, our soul, our mind, and our will.

Ponder the following text from Cyril of Alexandria. Note how Cyril affirms both Jesus' humanity and deity.

"You would yourself approve the correct and holy faith of those who so believe, if you would bring yourself to consider and to acknowledge that Christ is truly God, that he is one and is the only Son of the God and Father, not divided into God and man. You should say, rather, that he is one and the same, the Word from the Father, and man from a woman, just as we are, while he always remains God."[32]

This is a complex passage from Cyril, so let's unpackage it carefully. Cyril is responding to Nestorius, who at the time was archbishop of Constantinople. Nestorius was reluctant to call Mary *theotokos*, "the mother of God." He was willing to acknowledge Mary as the mother of Jesus' humanity, but not his deity. Of course, he was right, for Mary was not the source of Jesus' deity. God the Father was.

Yet Cyril was correct in believing that Nestorius erred in too sharply dividing Jesus' humanity from his divinity, for the one who was born of Mary was indeed God. As Cyril puts it in our quotation, "Christ is truly

---

32. Cyril of Alexandria, *Third Letter to Nestorius* (Letter 17); ACD2.130.

God...he is one and is the only Son of the God and Father, not divided into God and man."[33]

Cyril correctly insisted that Christ is one person – not two – and that his humanity and deity are perfectly united in an ineffable union in him. Hence, Mary should rightly be called "the mother of God," for the one person born of her was indeed *God* incarnate. To divide or separate Christ's humanity from his deity, as Nestorius seemed to do, threatened to obscure the wonder and beauty of Christ's incarnation, for the one born of Mary was indeed God the Son, who willingly joined his deity to the humanity offered to him by Mary. Jesus was fully God and fully human.

FULLY HUMAN

Jesus was and is fully human. Fully. Completely. He was not partly human and partly God. Jesus, the incarnate Son of God, is to this very day fully human and simultaneously fully God. A series of questions might prove helpful as we explore the beauty and wonder of Jesus:

Did Jesus Christ have a human mind?[34]

The short answer is "yes." Luke writes, for example, that Jesus "grew in wisdom and stature" (*Lk* 2:32). His mind developed as a human mind normally does, and so did his body. As a human baby, Jesus had the conceptual capabilities of a baby boy, then a child, then a teenager, then an adult. His human knowledge expanded as Jesus grew physically, emotionally, and spiritually.

Yet while Jesus' human mind developed and matured, he simultaneously possessed the divine mind of the second person of the Trinity, the eternal Son of God. It should not surprise us, then, that in Jesus' life and ministry he occasionally manifests knowledge only God could possess.

Hence, we concurrently affirm two truths: as the eternal Son of God, Jesus knew all things and never ceased to have this knowledge, for his

---

33. Ibid.
34. In the following material, I occasionally draw on ideas found in my book *A Different Way: Recentering the Christian Life on Following Jesus* (San Francisco, HarperOne, 2023), 86-95. I encourage readers to consult my more detailed treatment of the incarnation there.

mind was the mind of God. In his movement into our world in the incarnation, Jesus never ceased being God the Son, the second person of the holy Trinity. Jesus is fully God, fully human, and will always be so.

Yet as a human being with a fully functioning human mind, Jesus learned like humans learn. He learned carpentry from his father Joseph. He learned about the nature of wood, though he had created every tree on the surface of the earth! As Jesus practiced carpentry, his woodworking skills improved. A table built by Jesus at the age of eleven would differ from one he built at the age of twenty, for he was growing as a carpenter, just as he was growing as a human being.

Picture Jesus studying the Scripture. He heard it read and discussed by his parents and in his local synagogue. He read it. He memorized it. He recited it in synagogue. He discussed it in the family circle with Mary and Joseph. Yet as he grew in wisdom and stature, no doubt Mary and Joseph recognized abilities that vastly surpassed their own. Jesus' parents discovered him at age twelve in the synagogue discussing Torah with the teachers of Israel (*Lk* 2:46). Many in Israel began asking, who is this child with such profound questions and answers? People wondered. People pondered. We rightly do the same thing today.

The very one who inspired the Scripture now learns the Scripture! How strange! How wonderful! How mysterious! For Jesus was fully human, while never ceasing to exist as the eternal Son, fully divine.

Gregory of Nazianzus scolds those who doubt that Jesus' mind was fully human. "Anyone who has placed his hope in a human being who lacked a human mind is himself truly mindless and does not deserve a complete salvation. For what was not assumed was not healed. What is saved is that which has been united with God. If it was half of Adam that fell, then half might be assumed and saved. But if it was the whole of Adam that fell, it is united to the whole of him who was begotten and gains complete salvation."[35]

Did Jesus have a human soul? Yes, Jesus has a human soul. Why? Jesus must be all that we are – apart from sin -- *to save all that we are.* Jesus is saving our mind, our soul, our will, and our body. Why? All that we are as humans is *incurvatus in se*, bent and twisted. All that we are needs to be straightened out. So, to save us, the eternal Son of God assumes human

---

35. Gregory of Nazianzus, *Letter to Cledonius;* ACD 2.148.

nature. Jesus possesses all that characterizes us as humans, including a human soul. Just as we have souls that animate our bodies, so Jesus had a fully human soul that animated his body. If Jesus was soulless, he would not be fully human.

A human will? Yes, Jesus had a human will, as we all do. He freely made choices throughout his lifetime. For instance, Jesus chose twelve disciples, not thirteen or eleven. He chose how he would spend his time, what food he would eat, when he would get up in the morning and go to sleep at night, when and how he would pray and in what places. He never made a bad choice, for Jesus' will was not bent like ours. In his humanity, he never swerved from the will of his Father.

A human body? Did Jesus have a human body? Does he still have one today? This possibility was very hard for some ancient Christians to accept, especially those from a Greek or Roman background. Greek kids, for instance, grew up with Plato as a key teacher. They learned from him that human bodies hinder rather than help spiritual development. Have you ever felt the same way?

Plato referred to the body as a prison that the soul must escape to make its journey back to God. "*Soma sēma,*" Plato taught. "The body is a prison." Some Greek Christians, then, viewed the body as a hindrance to spiritual development and life. Known as Docetists, they reflected Plato's skepticism about the goodness of the body. They argued that Jesus only *seemed* (Gk. dokeo) to have a body. Note that this idea is not a Christian notion. It is an early Christian heresy.

The Nicene Creed firmly declares that the Son of God "became man." For now, remember that every characteristic of a male human body was true for Jesus's body. He slept, ate, breathed, had bowel movements, and so on. Jesus has, to this very day, a resurrected, human body. In his humanity, Jesus is a resurrected human being – mind, soul, will, and body.

Note, too, that Jesus shows his precious image-bearers that human embodiment is God's created will for us. Embodiment is not a mistake to be overcome; it is a blessing to be embraced. In a word, God loves bodies, just as God loves matter in general.

The next line of the creed turns our attention to the Virgin Mary.

11
VIRGIN BIRTH

... from the Virgin Mary, and was made man

*J*esus was born from the Virgin Mary. We read of Mary's encounter with the angel Gabriel in Luke 1:26-38. Take a moment to read this passage. God has sent the archangel Gabriel to Mary, a virgin pledged to be married to Joseph, a descendant of David.

"Greetings, you who are highly favored! The Lord is with you" (*Lk* 1:28). Gabriel's greeting "greatly troubled" Mary (*Lk* 1:29). Should we be surprised? Any woman would be troubled by such a greeting, especially one who had never had sexual relations with a man! Not only is Mary "troubled." She is afraid. Indeed, encountering an archangel is a terrifying experience. "Do not be afraid, Mary," Gabriel says, for Mary has "found favor with God" (*Lk* 1:30). How so?

Gabriel announces to Mary that she, though a virgin, "will conceive and give birth to a son, and you are to call him Jesus. He will be great and will be called the Son of the Most High. The Lord God will give him the throne of his father David, and he will reign over Jacob's descendants forever; his kingdom will never end" (*Lk* 1:31-33).

Mary is rightly puzzled; she understands the basics of human reproduction. "How will this be," Mary asks Gabriel, "since I am a virgin?" Quite clearly, Mary's question does not arise from a lack of faith. It is not like Zechariah's question in Luke 1:18. Zechariah posed his age as a problem to Gabriel's announcement that Zechariah's wife Elizabeth would have a child. Zechariah believed he and Elizabeth were simply too old for the promise to be fulfilled.

Yes, Mary asks Gabriel a question, but the narrative makes plain that Mary is receptive to God's work in her. She doesn't understand how a virgin can have children, but she is open to an explanation of this unique event. Never has a conception like this happened in human history. Never will it happen again.

Gabriel is careful to explain to Mary what will take place. He realizes Mary is confused, but not from a lack of faith. "The Holy Spirit will come on you, and the power of the Most High will overshadow you. So the holy one to be born will be called the Son of God" (*Lk* 1:35). Gabriel then informs Mary that her relative Elizabeth "is going to have a child in her old age . . . for no word from God will ever fail" (*Lk* 1:36-37).

How will Mary respond? Gabriel is asking permission on behalf of God to use Mary's womb to fulfill God's purposes and promises. It is Mary's decision to make, not Gabriel's. The narrative has reached its tensest point.

Mary answers with words that have echoed across hundreds and hundreds of years. "I am the Lord's servant," Mary answered. "May your word to me be fulfilled" (*Lk* 1:38).

Now let's study this passage from Luke with the help of the church fathers, especially with those from Africa. What themes do they notice in this text? And what do these themes imply for the words we have quoted from the Nicene Creed?

". . . **he became incarnate from the Virgin Mary, and was made man.**"

THE VIRGIN BIRTH

The comments of the church fathers on the virgin birth are interesting and insightful. The fathers always keep in mind both the divinity and humanity of Jesus, and how Jesus' birth from Mary fulfills the covenant promises made to David.

John McGuckin comments that from the church's beginning "Mary was an object of intense fascination and deep devotion to early Christians

... Devotion to Mary was important in Egypt, where the cult of the God-Mother Isis was progressively dislocated by the church's reattachment of popular devotion from the old gods and goddesses to the Savior and his mother."[1]

The person of Mary was extremely important in the christological controversies and clarifications that occurred after the formation of the Nicene Creed in the 4th century. McGuckin again is very helpful. "By the fifth century, the titles of Mary had come to feature centrally in the christological controversy . . . In each instance the figure of Mary the mother of the Lord is used to insist on the human reality of Jesus. When the church teaches that the incarnate Lord was the son of Mary, it is always shorthand for a rejection of the endlessly recurrent temptations to gnostic and docetic views that shied away, through various centuries, from the implications of his full acceptance of human fragility and limitation. The theology of the new Eve reflects what the church believes of the new Adam that issued from her."[2]

Hopefully, for all readers – Protestant, Catholic, and Orthodox – the insights of the African fathers on Jesus' mother will increase our love for God and the Holy Trinity's saving acts in the history of Israel and humanity at large.

Athanasius, for example, makes an interesting comparison between Aaron, Adam, and the Word. Aaron was not born a high priest. He was born as a man. "In the course of time," though, God willed that Aaron become a high priest. When this change occurred, Aaron received priestly garments, which he wore when "he entered into the holy place and offered the sacrifice to the people."[3] In a similar way, the Lord always was the eternal Word (*Jn* 1:1). Yet "when the Father willed that ransoms should be given for all and grace bestowed on all," the incarnation took place. Just as Aaron wore a robe to fulfill his vocation, "so the Word took earthly flesh, having Mary for the mother of his body. . ."[4]

Athanasius then inserts Adam into his discourse. For Adam had been made from "virgin soil." The incarnate Word, born of the virgin Mary, could then "offer himself to the Father and cleanse us from all sins. . . "

---

1. John McGuckin, ed., ACD 2.127.
2. Ibid.
3. Athanasius, *Against the Arians* 2.7.8; ACD 2.128.
4. Ibid.

Did the Word cease to be God by doing so? No. Just "as Aaron remained the same and did not change by assuming the high priest's dress . . .so the Lord did not become another by taking the flesh but remained clothed in it."[5]

Gregory of Nyssa comments that "the divine nature was implanted in both body and soul in corresponding measure and became united to both."[6] Gregory is specifically responding to Apollinaris, a man who taught that Jesus did not possess a human soul. No, Gregory writes. If Jesus did not have a human soul, he is not entirely human. And if he isn't entirely human, Jesus can't save all that we are, for all humans possess a soul. So, rather than using the language of replacement regarding Jesus' divinity, Gregory speaks of union. The divine nature of the Word was "united" to human nature. The compound nature of humans – mind, soul, will, and body – was united to the Word's divinity.

And what of Mary? Gregory writes that "in the case of the virgin birth the power of the Highest was implanted immaterially in the undefiled body and took the Virgin's purity as the material for the flesh."[7] God used Mary's undefiled body "toward the formation of one who was in truth a new man . . . created after the likeness of God, not in the fashion of humankind."[8] McGuckin comments: "Her blood nourished him, but he took the Virgin's purity to be the substance of the flesh he had made for himself."[9]

Keep this in mind: from the perspective of the church fathers, certain things must be true of Mary if she is to be the mother of Jesus, God incarnate. Mary feely and willingly offers her womb to God, a womb the church fathers consider to be absolutely virginal and pure. For as the Temple in Jerusalem was holy and pure, so will be God's new home in the womb of Mary.

THE MOTHER OF GOD OR THE MOTHER OF CHRIST?

A significant disagreement erupted in the fifth century CE between

---

5. Ibid.
6. Gregory of Nyssa, *Against Apollinaris* 54; ACD 2.128.
7. Ibid.
8. Ibid.
9. McGuckin, op. cit., 127.

Nestorius, the archbishop of Constantinople, and other key church fathers over the proper naming of Mary. At first glance it may seem unimportant, but the controversy is worth examining.

Nestorius believed Mary should be called *christotokos* (Gk.), for she was the mother of Christ, the promised Messiah. What Nestorius said was indeed true. Quite clearly, Mary was the mother of Jesus and Jesus was the promised anointed one, Israel's messiah. What Nestorius didn't want to call Mary is equally important, and drew heated responses from among a number of church fathers, chief among them the African Cyril of Alexandria.

Nestorius was opposed to calling Mary "the mother of God", or "God-bearer, *theotokos* in Greek. Initially, Nestorius seems correct. How could Mary give birth to God? Yet why the vigorous opposition among some to Nestorius's reluctance?

Thomas Oden explains: "The teaching of Nestorius did not receive ecumenical consent, but raised a decisive question for ecumenical teaching concerning Mary. The Nestorians were charged with asserting that there were two persons, a divine person distinguished from a human person, that this human person was conceived by the Virgin. The crisis emerged when Anastasius publicly denied to Mary the liturgically familiar title, 'Mother of God' (or bearer of God,' *Theotokos*) – the implication being that she was not mother of God but only of Christ (*Christotokos*) to whom the person of the Word of God had in some way united himself. This amounted to saying that Christ is two persons, one divine and one human, not one person with two natures. It was principally to guard the teaching of the distinctive unity of the Person of Jesus Christ against Nestorianism that 'Mother of God' was applied to Mary. Cyril of Alexandria and the Council of Ephesus (CE 431) cut through to the essential point, that the one born of the Virgin was Son of God at the time of his conception and birth."[10]

Gregory of Nazianzus, considered the greatest theologian in the East, comments that "Anyone who does not admit that holy Mary is the mother of God (*theotokos*) is out of touch with the Godhead."[11] Gregory's point is

---

10. Thomas C. Oden, *Classic Christianity: A Systematic Theology* (San Francisco: HarperOne, 1992), 295-296.
11. Gregory of Nazianzus, *Letter* 101.5. *To Cledonius;* ACD 2.129.

that it is God who was born of Mary, for it is God whose divine nature was joined to the human nature offered to God by Mary.

Cyril puts things very clearly. "I am amazed that there are some who are extremely doubtful whether the holy Virgin should be called mother of God or not. For if our Lord Jesus Christ is God, then surely the holy Virgin who have him birth must be God's mother."[12] Yes, the Word of God – God the Son – "is begotten of the substance of God the Father, as all acknowledge, and has his existence without beginning in time, always coexisting with his Father."[13] The eternal Son has no beginning and no end, and his divine nature has been joined to the human nature offered by the Virgin Mary.

In the incarnation, when the eternal Word of God "became flesh, that is, and was united with flesh endowed with a rational soul, he is said also to have been begotten through a woman according to the flesh."[14] Cyril is deeply concerned that Nestorius's position weakens the church's understanding that Christ is genuinely God. "You would yourself approve the correct and holy faith of those who so believe, if you would bring yourself to consider and to acknowledge that Christ is truly God, that he is one and is the only Son of the God and Father, not divided into God and man. You should say, rather, that he is one and the same, the Word from the Father, and man from a woman, just as we are, while he always remains God."[15]

Do you see Cyril's point? If Mary is only described as the mother of the Messiah, *christotokos* as Nestorius puts it, people will fail to grasp the wonder and glory of Christ's person. The child "the holy Virgin brought forth, after the flesh, God personally united to flesh, for this reason we say of her that she is mother of God (*theotokos*) . . . the Virgin is called *theotokos* because having personally united man's nature to himself, the Word accepted even to be born in the flesh, from her womb."[16]

To sum up, the baby born of Mary was fully human and fully God. Jesus is Emmanuel, God with us. "God the Word became incarnate, and

---

12. Cyril of Alexandria, *Letter 1, To the Monks of Egypt*; ACD 2.129.
13. Ibid.
14. Cyril of Alexandria, *Against Nestorius* 1.1; ACD 2.130.
15. Ibid.
16. Cyril of Alexandria, *Third Letter to Nestorius* (Letter 17); ACD 2.130.

from the very conception united to himself the temple taken from her."[17] Mary is indeed the new Temple, for the one conceived in her was God incarnate.

MARY AS THE NEW EVE

We all know the tragic story, the horror that broke loose in the garden of Eden. The devil tempts Eve, and she succumbs. Eve takes and eats. And human nature disintegrates.

Happily, Eve's sin was not the end of the story. Yes, as the African Tertullian writes, the "devil had taken captive the image and likeness of God." Yet God responds by restoring "the image by a parallel process."[18] Tertullian then develops the redemptive parallel. Negatively, we have the devil's tempting word: "For the word that was the architect of death found its way into the ear of Eve while she was still virgin." In redemptive response, "the Word of God, which was the builder of life, had to be introduced into a virgin, so that what had gone to destruction through the female sex should be restored to salvation."[19]

Ponder these important parallels:

- Eve believes the serpent.
- Mary believes Gabriel.

- Eve sins by believing a devilish word.
- Mary obediently believes a redemptive word.

- Eve later gives birth "as an outcast...and in sorrow." Indeed, the child Eve bears "is a devil who murdered his brother."[20] Mary gives birth to one "who should in time bring salvation to Israel, his own brother after the flesh..."[21]

- God sends into Mary's womb "his Word, the good brother, that

---

17. Cyril of Alexandria, *Letter* 39, *To John of Antioch (The Formula of Reunion);* ACD 2.131.
18. Tertullian, *On the Flesh of Christ* 17; ACD 2.133.
19. Ibid.
20. Ibid.
21. Ibid.

he might wipe out the memory of the wicked brother. It was necessary that Christ should come forth for humankind's salvation from that place into which humankind had entered when already condemned."[22]

AND WAS MADE MAN

Ancient Christians struggled to make sense out of the incarnation. Consider three interpretive options, the third of which was declared by the Nicene Creed to be true:

- *Jesus was not fully divine*, but an elevated creature of some sort.

- *Jesus was not fully human*. Some believed that though Jesus appeared to be a human being, he had no soul. The followers of Apollinaris made this very error. Augustine mentions that they "wrongly supposed that the man Christ either had no soul or had no rational soul."[23] Augustine's teaches that if Jesus did not possess a rational soul, he was not a human being, for all humans possess souls.

- Jesus was fully human and fully divine.

Consider this comment of John McGuckin and ponder it carefully: ". . . the radical commitment to the double notions of perfect Godhead and perfect manhood for the one incarnate Lord was a confession of faith that troubled the fourth and fifth centuries of the church in a deep way. It might even today be said to be the central question of christological faith. The great Nicene teachers come back time and time again to the profound paradox that the incarnation represents."[24]

Carefully ponder the Nicene phrase "he was made man." It attests to the genuine reality of both Jesus' humanity and his deity. Athanasius is at pains to teach that the divine Word, the *logos*, did not dwell in Jesus like

---

22. Ibid; ACD 2.134.
23. Augustine, *Letter* 140.12; ACD 2.139.
24. McGuckin, ACD 2.137.

the Word indwells other humans. No, the divine Word became incarnate, and bore every characteristic of a human male. "He became man, and did not come into a man. We must be clear about this, to avoid the notion that the Word dwelled in a man, hallowing him and displaying himself in him, as in earlier times the Word came to each of the saints."[25]

Do we comprehend how Jesus can be both fully human and fully God? Absolutely not. Such a proposition seems self-contradictory. For can a human simultaneously possess the attributes of God, while also possessing the attributes of a human being? We don't know how this is possible. Yet, as Athanasius sees clearly, this is the paradox that must be maintained. If we reduce either Jesus's divinity or humanity, the logical tension the paradox presents disappears, and in turn our salvation is imperiled. "In that case, there would have been no paradox, and those who saw him would not have been startled . . . for 'the Word became flesh' (*Jn* 1:14) as John says, and in Scripture 'flesh' is commonly used for 'man.'"[26]

Tertullian helpfully comments that "Jesus consisted of flesh and spirit; of flesh as man, of Spirit as God. The angel at the time proclaimed him Son of God, in respect that he was Spirit, keeping for the flesh the title Son of man. Thus also the apostle confirms that he was composed of two realities, when he designated him the 'mediator of God and people'" (1 Tim 2:5)."[27] Two realities indeed! Spirit and human nature joined in an incomprehensible, wondrous union.

Tertullian understands clearly that the Son of God became what we are – while remaining what he was – for our sake and out of love for us. Some Christians thought it was unseemly or shameful for God to be born, to take such a humiliating step into our world by becoming what we are. But that is just the point.

> Take away the process of birth, and then show me the person. Take away the flesh and then show me whom Christ redeemed. If these constitute those whom God redeemed, how can you represent them as humiliating to him, seeing that he redeemed them?[28]

---

25. Athanasius, *Against the Arians* 3.30; ACD 2.138.
26. Ibid.
27. Tertullian, *Against Praxeas* 27; ACD 2.140.
28. Tertullian, *On the Flesh of Christ* 4; ACD 2.140.

People such as Marcion of Sinope, Tertullian comments, disparaged a true incarnation because he didn't understand the gospel and its dynamic. The incarnation was a glorious event for the Son of God. Through the incarnation and its various aspects, Jesus saved humanity in its entirety.

> He reforms our birth by a new birth from heaven. He restores our flesh from all that afflicts it. He cleanses it when leprous, gives it new light when blind, new strength when paralyzed, exorcizes it when possessed by demons, and even raises it to life when dead. So what humiliation was there in being born in flesh?[29]

Though Jesus Christ possesses two natures – one human and one divine – he is not two different people, one God and one human. As Cyril of Alexandria notes, we do "not divide the one Son into two, God forbid, but only insofar as to confess that there occurred neither confusion nor mixing..."[30] Cyril's point is that divine nature and human nature were not mixed or blended in the incarnation. No, The Son remained fully God. Yet in the incarnation God's nature was joined to human nature in an ineffable union. Here we have union, not a mixing or blending into a third sort of creature.

Cyril sums things up nicely

> We say that the unique Word of God, who was begotten of the very substance of the Father, who is true God of true God, the Light of Light, through whom all things came into being, both things in heaven and things in earth, coming down for the sake of our salvation and humbling himself even to emptying (cf. *Phil* 2:5-11), was made flesh and became man. That is, taking flesh of the holy Virgin and making it his own from the womb, he underwent a birth like ours and came forth a man of woman, not throwing off what he was, but even though he became man by the assumption of flesh and blood, yet still remaining what he was, that is, God indeed in nature and truth.[31]

---

29. Ibid.
30. Cyril of Alexandria, *Letter to Eulogius;* ACD 2.140.
31. Cyril of Alexandria, *Third Letter to Nestorius* (Letter 17); ACD 2.140.

* * *

Pause and Reflect: Pause for a moment and reread what I have just quoted from Cyril. Pray for understanding of the dynamic of the incarnation. Again, God is not changed into a human being. No, God in the person of the eternal Son joins his divine nature to human nature in a union we simply cannot comprehend but surely can worship. Cyril again is helpful. "We do not say that the flesh was changed into the nature of Godhead or that the ineffable nature of the Word of God was transformed into the nature of flesh, for he is unchangeable and unalterable, always remaining the same according to the Scriptures."[32]

* * *

I find the poetry of Ephrem the Syrian to be helpful, for he poetically captures the beauty of the incarnation. "Who will measure you, great Sea who made himself small? We came to see you as God. Behold! You are a human being. We came to see you as a human being, and lo! The banner of your Godhead shines forth. Who can bear your transformations, O true One?"[33]

A TREASURE CHEST OF JEWELS

Picture the incarnation as a multifaceted diamond. We have been enjoying the facets that especially pertain to *who it was* that entered our world as Jesus of Nazareth. Now take the diamond in your fingers, hold it up to the light, and see how other facets reveal themselves, beauties that *reflect why God became incarnate*. Imagine yourself opening an incarnation treasure chest. As I list aspects of the incarnation, drop each jewel into the chest.

Let's start by turning our attention to Gregory of Nazianzus, the great Cappadocian father. Why did God become human? He did so to "remove the curse from me" and "was called a curse on my account; he who takes

---

32. Ibid.
33. Ephrem the Syrian, *Hymns on the Nativity* 13.7-9; ACD 2.142.

away the sin of the world was called sin. And he becomes the new Adam to take the place of the old."[34]

- Jewel One – Christ removed the curse from me.
- Jewel Two – Christ was called a curse on my account.
- Jewel Three – Christ takes away the sin of the world.
- Jewel Four – Christ was called sin.
- Jewel Five – Christ as the new Adam replaces the old.

Clement of Alexandria teaches that "The Lord, as God and man, gives us all kinds of profit and help. As God he forgives our sins; as man he educates us to be free from sin."[35]

- Jewel Six – As God, the Lord forgives our sin.
- Jewel Seven – As man, he teaches us how to obey, how to be free from sin.

Let's continue to fill the treasure chest. Cyril of Alexandria has a number of jewels for us.

Cyril writes that the Word became incarnate "so he could make his own that human flesh that was subject to corruption and sick with its desires and destroy corruption within it, since he is Life and Lifegiver, bringing its innate impulses to order. This was how the sin that lay within it was to be put to death, for we remember how the blessed Paul called our innate impulses the law of sin (*Rom* 7:23). From the time that human flesh became the personal flesh of the Word it has ceased to be subject to corruption, and since he who dwelled within it and revealed it as his very own, knew no sin being God . . . it has also ceased to be sick with its desires. The only-begotten Word of God did not bring this about for his own benefit, for he is ever what he is, but evidently he did if for ours. And if we were subject to the evils following from Adam's transgression then Christ's benefit also must come to us, that is, incorruption and the putting to death of sin. This is why he became man."[36]

---

34. Gregory of Nazianzus, *Oration* 30.5; ACD 2.142.
35. Clement of Alexandria, *Christ the Educator* 1.3. (7); ACD 2.142.
36. Cyril of Alexandria, *First Letter to Succensus* 9; ACD 2.143.

This is a long passage. Now let's mine it for its gems. Each one of them reflects the wonder and beauty of the incarnation.

- Jewel Eight – As Life and Lifegiver, the incarnate Word in union with human nature has destroyed the corruption we have inherited from Adam.
- Jewel Nine – Through the power of the incarnate Word, human nature's innate disordered impulses, "the law of sin" (*Rom* 7:23), are brought to order.
- Jewel Ten – Human flesh – human nature – is now "the personal flesh of the Word."
- Jewel Eleven – Since human nature has been joined to the Word, who knew no sin, "it has ceased to be subject to corruption," and "ceased to be sick with its desires." This jewel resembles jewel eight.
- Jewel Twelve – All these wonders have been done for our benefit.
- Jewel Thirteen – Every evil we inherited from Adam has been overcome through the incarnation. "This is why he became man."

Now gather all these jewels in the treasure chest of your mind. Allow them meditatively to descend from your mind into your heart. Gaze upon them there. Can you see them sparkling in your heart, radiating light into every nook and cranny of your being?

Jesus Christ, genuinely, fully human, genuinely, fully divine. Cyril points to "the blameless human passions" that Jesus experienced such as "sleepiness", "anxiety", and "pain" as markers of Jesus' true humanity, "that we might believe that he did become man." We can be assured that Jesus understands and has experienced the human condition.[37]

Yet, Cyril teaches, Jesus also performed miracles in his earthly ministry that demonstrate his deity. In contrast with his humanity, "to assure those who saw that he was truly God, as well as being man, he worked divine signs, rebuking the sea, raising the dead, and performing other wonderful works. He even endured the cross so that by suffering death in the flesh

---

37. Ibid.

(though not in the nature of the Godhead), he might become 'he firstborn from the dead' (*Col* 1:18)."[38]

Jesus now serves as our unique high priest to God the Father. Cyril comments on Hebrews 3:1, ". . . he ministers to God the Father that confession of faith that we offer both to him and through him to God the Father (and certainly to the Holy Spirit also). We also confess that he is by nature the only-begotten Son of God, and that we do not attribute the priesthood, both the name and the thing, to another man beside him."[39] Christ's status as the high priest of the Christian community is utterly unique. "For he has become a 'mediator between God and people, and the one who reconciles us to peace, since he has offered up himself as a smell of sweet savor to God the Father' (1 *Tim* 2:5)."[40]

The incarnation is real, rooted in history; it took place in Judea in the first century CE. Why do I stress this? Some ancient Christians – like some modern ones – were tempted to view Jesus as a phantasm or ghost. They believed Jesus looked like a human being, but really wasn't. He only seemed to be.

Athanasius considered such an idea utter nonsense, for a ghostly Jesus couldn't help anyone, much less accomplish the salvation of the world.

> For when the Savior really and in truth became man, salvation was effected for the whole of humankind. If, as they say, the Word was only in the body notionally, and this notion is said to be a phantasm, then the so-called salvation and resurrection of humanity will also be found to have taken place merely in semblance . . . But our salvation is no imaginary thing; nor is it the body only, but in reality the whole person, both body and soul, which has attained to salvation in the Word.[41]

Be encouraged by Athanasius's words. In Christ, all that you are as a human being has been saved. Your body has been saved. Your soul has been saved. Your mind has been saved. Your will has been saved.

Some ancient Christians were sorely tempted to over-spiritualize salvation. We sometimes see this tendency in modern Christian circles.

---

38. Ibid.
39. Cyril of Alexandria, *Third Letter to Nestorius* (Letter 13); ACD 2.143.
40. Ibid.
41. Athanasius, *Letter to Epictetus* 7; ACD 2.144-145.

"God came to save souls," an evangelist might preach. No, Athanasius would respond. God is more earthy than that. God came to save human beings, soul and body.

Again, we turn to the poems and hymns of Ephrem the Syrian. Ephrem was entranced by what God did in the incarnation. Who would have thought that God could become human, while never ceasing to be God?

> Blessed is the Unlimited who was limited! Your majesty is hidden from us; your grace is revealed before us . . . Your grace made you a babe; your grace made you a human being. Your majesty contracted and stretched out. Blessed is the power that became small and became great! Glory to him who became earthly although heavenly by his nature . . . He became by his will a human, although he is God by his nature . . . Glorious is your will and your nature. Glorious is your will and your nature! . . . Blessed is he who became young and restored youth to all . . . Your birth became for the hopeless a spring gushing hope. Blessed is that hope that brought the gospel.[42]

* * *

Pause and Reflect: Prayerfully ponder the last line of the hymn. "Blessed is that hope that brought the gospel." For many Christians, the gospel means that Jesus died for our sins on the cross. That statement is surely true. What Ephrem understands, along with all the African fathers, is captured in his hymn. For Jesus to die for our sins, God has to accomplish the seemingly impossible. The unlimited, as Ephrem puts it, had to become limited. In your mind picture the baby Jesus nestled in the womb of the Virgin Mary. That is God incarnate nestled there, simultaneously occupying all space and time. Ephrem sings that "your birth became mother of all creatures, since, again, she labored and gave birth to humanity which gave birth to you. Humanity gave birth to you physically; you begot her spiritually. Your birth became begetter of all."[43] Pray and

---

42. Ephrem the Syrian, *Hymns on the Nativity* 23.2-6; ACD 2.145.
43. Ibid.

ponder over this poetry from Ephraim. Write down two or three insights or encouragements that come to mind.

*　*　*

Cyril of Alexandria exults in the same wonder and beauty as Ephrem. "Do not simply look on him who was laid in the manger as a mere babe, but in our poverty see him who as God is rich, and in the measure of our humanity him who excels the inhabitants of heaven. This is why he is glorified even by the holy angels."[44]

No longer are we the enemies of God.

> But Christ has abolished all this. He is our peace, for he himself has united us to God the Father, 'having taken away from the middle the cause of the enmity, which is sin' (*Eph* 2:14), and so justifies us by faith, and makes us holy and without blame and calls us near to him when we were once afar off. . . Christ, therefore, has been made for us both peace and goodwill, by whom and with whom to God the Father be glory and honor and might with the Holy Spirit, to the ages of ages. Amen.[45]

The man could preach!

We listen to Cyril and are reminded of Tom Oden's vivid metaphor regarding the teaching of the church fathers. "Watching them play theology is like watching Willie Mays play centerfield or Duke Ellington play 'Sophisticated Lady' . . . So cool it, relax, breathe, and swim to the deep fathoms."[46]

Cyril summarizes the gospel in the series of sermons he preached on the gospel of Luke.

> God in his love to humankind provided for us a way of salvation and of life. For believing in the Father, Son and Holy Spirit and making this confession before many witnesses, we wash away all the filth of sin, and

---

44. Cyril of Alexandria, *Homilies on the Gospel of Luke* 2; ACD 2.146.
45. Ibid.
46. Thomas C. Oden, *Classic Christianity*, xviii.

are enriched by the communication of the Holy Spirit, and 'are made partakers of the divine nature' (2 *Pet* 1:4) and gain the grace of adoption.[47]

Did you notice the connection Cyril makes between "salvation and life"? Salvation brings us life, a life patterned on the self-sacrifice of Jesus. Jesus is "the pattern and way of every good work. For it follows that 'he who in everything is first' (*Rom* 8:29) must in this also set the example."[48]

The skill with which Cyril speaks of Christ's deity and humanity is striking. He fully emphasizes both, with each retaining all its characteristics. "The Word endured to be born in human fashion, although in his divine nature he has no beginning and is subject to no time."[49] Cyril then describes the beautiful paradoxes of the incarnation. "He who as God is all perfect submits to bodily growth. The incorporeal One has limbs that advance to the ripeness of manhood. He is filled with wisdom who is himself all wisdom."[50]

* * *

Pause and Reflect: Take time to ponder the incarnational paradoxes Cyril presents. A warning bell should go off in your mind if these paradoxes are absent from your thinking – and perhaps teaching – about Jesus. For Jesus as fully God and fully human must be true if we are to be saved. What insights and questions arise in your mind? List them.

* * *

THE BLESSING OF JESUS AS FULLY HUMAN

Let's pause for a moment to consider the blessing of Jesus as fully human. It is encouraging to do so. When was the last time you were tempted? Five minutes ago? Temptation can be so discouraging, and the battle against sin fatiguing and depressing.

How can Jesus as *fully* human help us? Origen helpfully comments:

---

47. Cyril of Alexandria, *Homilies on the Gospel of Luke* 11; ACD 2.147.
48. Ibid.
49. Cyril of Alexandria, *Homilies on the Gospel of Luke* 5; ACD 2.147-148.
50. Ibid.

"The Lord when he took flesh was tempted by every temptation by which human beings are to be tempted. He was tempted for this purpose, that we might overcome through his victory. . ."[51] Think of that. Jesus was tempted for our sake. We can participate in his victory by clinging to him. Our struggles are not foreign to him, for he himself experienced – and overcame – temptation.

Some ancient Christians struggled to believe Jesus was fully human because they feared our sinfulness might infect his divine nature. Augustine addresses this concern in his work *On the Agony of Christ*. "Those people do not know that the substance of God, which directs the whole creation, is utterly incapable of being contaminated."[52]

Augustine observes that the sun's rays are not soiled when they shine on dirt or corruption. They contact impurity yet "escape contamination." So it is with "the invisible and unchangeable Truth to avoid pollution when it freed humanity from all its infirmities by assuming the whole man; man's spirit, and, in consequence, man's soul, and, in consequence, man's body."[53] Human nature in its entirety has been assumed and healed by the incarnate Son of God, Jesus Christ.

In *The City of God*, Augustine explains the dynamic of the incarnation. He writes that the "Son of God" pitied us and became what we are. Why? ". . . so that we who are mortal by nature might, through him, become children of God by grace."[54] Did God the eternal Son cease being God when he became a human being? Absolutely not.

> *While remaining unchangeable,* he assumed from us our nature, so that he could assume us through it. *While holding on to his divinity,* he came to share in our weakness, so that we might change for the better, through our participation in his immortality and righteousness, by shedding what is sinful and mortal in us and preserving the good that he did through our nature, after that good had been filled with the highest good through the goodness of his nature.[55]

---

51. Origen, *Homily on the Gospel of Luke* 29; ACD 2.148.
52. Augustine, *On the Agony of Christ* 20; ACD 2.151.
53. Ibid.
54. Augustine, *The City of God* 7.3; ACD 2.153.
55. Ibid., my emphasis.

In this utterly unique movement into human history, God the Son remains what he is while becoming what we are, apart from sin. This is Jesus, the incarnate Son. His human nature was not twisted and bent like ours, so that he could straighten us out. His deity was not mixed with his humanity; Jesus is not some third thing, neither human nor divine. No, Jesus was and is fully God and fully human, each nature distinct yet in everlasting union. As such, Christ's divine nature communicates its benefits to the human nature he has assumed. In union with him, "in Christ," "through the righteousness given by one human who was also God," we attain "that good that is so exalted."[56]

Jesus, indeed, is Emmanuel, "God with us." Arnobius the Younger captures the dynamic of the incarnation beautifully. "He comes to us through what he assumed from us and liberates us by that means, insofar as he aways remained in his own station."[57]

Athanasius, too, is helpful. "But from Mary the Word took flesh and came forth as man, being in his nature and essence the Word of God, but according to the flesh made man, as Paul said, from the seed of David and the flesh of Mary (Rom 1:3)."[58]

Cyril of Alexandria carefully describes the wonder and beauty of God as Emmanuel – "God with us" – and explains that for God to be with us in this way is beautiful and unexpected. For, Cyril writes, "Divinity and flesh are by nature diverse in kind. . ." Yet in the incarnation, "the Word's body was his own; the Word united to that body was not separated from it. This is the only way in which we should conceive of Emmanuel, 'God with us.'"[59]

Note carefully that these two natures – divine and human – are "diverse in kind." One would not expect it was possible that this diversity could be joined in a genuine union, but that is exactly what has happened in the incarnation.

Because the two natures are joined in Christ – "inseparably conjoined" as Athanasius puts it --something as simple and commonplace as Jesus' spittle possessed divine power. "He spat in human fashion, but his spittle

---

56. Ibid.
57. Arnobius the Younger, *Conflict with Serapion* 2.31; ACD 2.154.
58. Athanasius, *Letter to Epictetus* 11-12; ACD 2.155.
59. Cyril of Alexandria, *Against Nestorius* 2 (Preface); ACD 2.155.

had divine power, for by it he restored sight to the eyes of the man blind from birth."[60]

Remember, too, that Mary should be called the mother of God, "since she gave birth to God made flesh and made man."[61] Cyril rebuked Nestorius's hesitancy to call Mary the mother of God; he discerned that Nestorius's reluctance threatened the wonder of what God was doing in Christ. Yes, the Lord was the Messiah, as Nestorius emphasized. Mary gave birth to the Christ, the *christotokos*. But the purposes of God were even deeper. God was joining deity to human nature, to save human nature from its sinful infection. Sin was killing us, and God in Christ came to save us from death and destruction.[62]

Christ is one -- a single person.

> . . . he is not twofold; he is one single Lord and Son, the Word of God the Father, in the flesh. I myself acknowledge that there is a very great difference, indeed the greatest disparity, between divinity and humanity. These terms clearly denote things essentially diverse and utterly dissimilar. But when the mystery of Christ is presented to us, then the principle of unity does not ignore the difference, but it excludes division. It does not confuse the natures. The Word of God partook of flesh and blood, and the Son is conceived of as one and is so named.[63]

Note that Cyril calls the incarnation "the mystery of Christ." He never says we will comprehend this mystery. For it is incomprehensible. If we applied the rules of logic to the incarnation, we no doubt would conclude that the incarnation can't possibly occur, for how can God become human while remaining God? We worship the mystery, rather than comprehend it.

* * *

Pause and Reflect: Here is a key point to ponder. The church fathers don't explain the incarnation. Rather, they build a transparent wall

---

60. Athanasius, *Letter to Serapion* 4.14; ACD 2.156.
61. Cyril of Alexandria, *First Letter to Succensus* 4; ACD 2.156.
62. Ibid.
63. Cyril of Alexandria, *Against Nestorius* 2.6; ACD 2.158.

around it, telling us what it isn't and allowing what it is to fill our minds and hearts. We don't comprehend the mystery; we worship it. So, in Jesus we recognize and worship two natures in one person. "All the terms used in the Gospels are to be referred to one person . . . There is one Lord Jesus Christ, according to the Scripture."[64] What insights and questions come to you as you ponder the incarnation? Write down two or three.

* * *

Ancient Christian teachers used various metaphors or similes to illustrate the union of divinity with humanity in Christ. Origen, for instance, proposes the metaphor of iron in fire. "If then some mass of iron is put into the fire, it receives heat in all its pores and veins and becomes wholly fire, if it never leaves the fire or is taken from it."[65] In a similar way, the human nature of Jesus, in union with the fire of his divinity, begins to glow. It never changes completely into the divine, but the union is intimate.[66]

To use Cyril's language,

> we affirm that the Word personally united to himself flesh animated with living soul in an ineffable and inconceivable manner and thereby became man and was called Son of man . . . It was not as though the diversity of the natures was done away by this union, but rather Godhead and Manhood completed for us the one Lord and Christ and Son by their unutterable and unspeakable concurrence into unity.[67]

* * *

Pause and Reflect: Tuck away in your memory Cyril's reminder that the incarnation is "ineffable," "inconceivable," "unutterable," "unspeakable," and was "completed for us." God loves us with a wondrous, beautiful love, and the incarnation is the proof. . .The Word was made flesh" (*Jn* 1:14). "And that means precisely that he became partaker of flesh and blood, just

---

64. Cyril of Alexandria, *Third Letter to Nestorius* (Letter 17); ACD 2.157.
65. Origen, *On First Principles* 2.6.6; ACD 2.159.
66. Ibid.
67. Cyril of Alexandria, *Letter to Nestorius* (Letter 4); ACD 2.160.

as we do, and made our body his own. He issued as man from a woman, but he did not cast off his being God and his generation from God the Father. He assumed our flesh, but even in doing this he remained what he was."[68] What new insights for you arise from Cyril's teaching? If you were having dinner with him, what would you like to ask him? List your questions.

***

The *simultaneity* of the incarnation is clear. What do I mean? The incarnate Christ is simultaneously fully God and fully human. The church fathers repeatedly emphasize this. This is extremely important for us to remember, for Christians past and present can find the incarnation to be confusing. Why? We can't make logical sense of it. As Cyril mentions in the passage I just quoted, Jesus "issued as man from a woman" – he's fully human – while "he did not cast off his being God and his generation from God the Father. He assumed our flesh, *but even in this he remained what he was*" (my emphasis).

Listen to the African Cyril beat the drum of simultaneity:

> For he wished to become man without casting off his natural being as God, and even when he descended into our limitations and put on the form of the slave, even so he remained in the transcendent condition of the Godhead and in his natural state as Lord.[69]

> We confess, therefore, our Lord Jesus Christ... born of the Virgin Mary, as touching his manhood; the same of one substance with the Father as touching his Godhead, and of one substance with us as touching his manhood. For of two natures a union has been made. For this cause we confess one Christ, one Son, one Lord.[70]

It's important that we get the incarnation right. I've run across Christians who believe that when the Son became a human male he stop being

---

68. Ibid., ACD 2.161.
69. Cyril of Alexandria, *First Letter to Succensus* 5; ACD 2.163.
70. Cyril of Alexandria, *Letter 39, To John of Antioch (The Formula of Reunion)*; ACD 2.163.

God. So let's be very clear about this, for the church fathers emphasize this point. God can't stop being God. This is an impossibility. That little baby in the manger, waiting to be nursed by his mother Mary, continues to reign over the universe as God.

When Jesus spoke as a human he was teaching as God -- and as a human being. As Cyril of Alexandria writes,

> But when seen as a babe and wrapped in swaddling clothes, even when still in the bosom of the Virgin who bore him, he filled all creation as God and was enthroned with him who begot him. For the divine cannot be numbered or measured and does not admit of circumscription.[71]

Ponder Cyril's last point, for it was a very important one for the African fathers. Then listen carefully to Origen: "The Savior sometimes speaks concerning himself as a man, sometimes as concerning a more divine nature, a nature that is one with the uncreated nature of the Father. When he says, 'Now you seek to kill me, a man who has spoken the truth to you' (Jn 8:40), he says this knowing that what they sought to destroy was not God but man. But in saying, 'I and the Father are one' (Jn 10:30), 'I am the truth and the life' (Jn 14:6), and 'I am the resurrection' (Jn 11:25), he is not teaching them about the man whom the Jews sought to destroy. . . 'You know me, and I know where I am' (Jn 7:28) is said of himself as man, while 'You know neither me nor my Father' (Jn 8:19) of his Godhead.[72]

Origen is concerned to distinguish between sayings or actions of Jesus that reflect his humanity, and others that reflect his deity. This will continue to be of great interest to other African church fathers such as Athanasius and Cyril of Alexandria.

The church fathers realized that biblical interpretation is an art that demands of the artist a palette possessing the colors of both Christ's deity and humanity. Over time, as biblical interpreters immersed their interpretive awareness in the mystery of the incarnation, their ability to interpret the meaning of Scripture broadened and deepened.

The meaning of the incarnate Jesus – think of his teaching and his actions -- is difficult to interpret because the union of his humanity and

---

71. Cyril of Alexandria, *Third Letter to Nestorius* (Letter 17); ACD 2.170.
72. Origen, *Commentary on the Gospel of John* 19.2. (1); ACD 2.167.

his divinity naturally influences whatever he says or does, for he is a single person. Unlike us -- his precious image-bearers -- he has two natures while we have only one.

Cyril recognizes that we must keep the "economy" in mind as we read the Gospels, or we will be confused by what Jesus is saying or doing. By "economy" Cyril means God's plan and actions in human history to overcome sin, evil, and death. Some texts refer to God's "economy" and distinguish between Jesus' deity and his humanity.

Cyril writes, "For this reason he sometimes speaks economically as man, in human fashion, and at other times, as God, he makes statements with divine authority."[73] In his letter to John of Antioch, Cyril makes this very point:

> As for the utterances about the Lord in the Gospels and apostolic writings, we know that the theologians regard some as common to both natures on the basis of one person, and others they distinguish, on the basis of two natures, referring the godlike utterances to the divinity of Christ and the lowly to his humanity.[74]

It is time to draw Volume Two to a close. It is available directly from ICCS Press, or Amazon. My prayer is that as you continue to plumb the wonder and beauty of the incarnation, your mind and heart will be nourished, your faith be enlivened, and your life with Christ be deepened. May God bless you this day and forevermore.

---

73. Cyril of Alexandria, *First Letter to Succensus* 6; ACD 2.165. My emphasis.
74. Cyril of Alexandria, *Letter 39, To John of Antioch (The Formula of Reunion)*; ACD 2.165.

ABOUT THE AUTHOR

Christopher A. Hall, former President of Renovaré, was Director of Academic Spiritual Formation and Distinguished Professor of Theology at Eastern University. Chris is the author of a number of books, including *The Mystery of God* (with Steven D. Boyer; Baker Academic), *Reading Scripture with the Church Fathers* (IVP Academic), *Learning Theology with the Church Fathers* (IVP Academic), *Worshiping with the Church Fathers* (IVP Academic), *Living Wisely with the Church Fathers* (IVP Academic), and *The Trinity* (with Roger Olson; Eerdmans). His most recent book is *A Different Way: Recentering the Christian Life Around Following Jesus* (HarperOne). Chris and his wife Debbie reside in Malvern, PA. They have three grown children and three grandchildren.

COVER ARTIST

Yoseph Abate was born in Bahir Dar, in 1978, graduated from the Alle School of Fine Arts and Design in 1996.

CAREER AND EXHIBITIONS:

He has participated in several group and solo Art Exhibitions in Ethiopia. His Art Exhibitions: Alle School of Fine Arts and Design (1996 Group), Imperial Hotel (1997, 1998), ECA (1998, 2000), Goshu Art Gallery (1998, 2002 Group), Alliance Ethio-Francaise (1999 Group), Sheraton Addis (2000 Group), Hilton AA (2007, 2008), The 27 European Capitals Painting Exhibition at Alliance Ethio-Francaise (2009 Group), Sodere Art Studio (2012), Hilton AA (2013 Group) National museum (2013, 2014 group), and Sheraton Addis (2017, 2019 group). Find other artwork created by Yoseph at https://fineartamerica.com/profiles/yoseph-abate

www.ingramcontent.com/pod-product-compliance
Lightning Source LLC
Chambersburg PA
CBHW070141080526
44586CB00015B/1787